THE HARDTALK
HANDBOOK

COPYRIGHT

This edition first published 2018

Registered Office:

Powerful Developing Services Institute (PDSi)
101-27 Regalia Business Center, 1st Floor, Building 3,
Bay Square, Business Bay
P.O.Box 390667, Dubai
United Arab Emirates

All rights reserved. No part of this publication may be reproduced, stored in a retrieval system, or transmitted, in any form or by any means, electronic, mechanical, photocopying, recording or otherwise without the prior permission of the publisher.

Designations used by companies to distinguish their products are often claimed as trademarks. All brand names and product names used in this book are trade names, service marks, trademarks or registered trademarks of their respective owners. This publication is designed to provide accurate and authoritative information in regard to the subject matter covered.

ISBN Number 9781727046205

POEM

NOW YOU'RE TALKING

Most often referred to as the 'Poet Laureate of Twitter', Brian Bilston is as mysterious as he is talented. His love of playful language is only equalled by his distaste for Jeremy Clarkson (let's just say we're glad he likes us). Much like our author, he can be found most days on the blue bird of social media and can be bribed into interaction with bike clips and Vimto. Here is his poetic take on HardTalk:

I – In which the poet writes a poem

Small talk is easy
whether you're discussing the weather or the TV.
But what if there are other words that float in your head
which always remain unsaid?

Words you always wanted to say
but could never find the optimum way
Conversations you end up sweeping under the carpet.
You'd like to begin one but you're unsure how to start it.

If only you could utilise the correct tools,
learn a new way, find a set of rules
to enable you to have difficult conversations
without offence or obfuscation.

II – In which the poet learns some hard truths

*Thanks for sharing this poem with me;
I have been giving it some thought.
There's much to like. The spelling's good.
The font is clear. It's mercifully short.*

*But I have some ideas to share
which I think will help improve it.*

*Those idioms don't travel well.
And the jargon jars: remove it.*

*Think about the pace and rhythm
and how to make the poem scan.
The ending could be stronger still.
Thanks. I do hope you understand.*

III – In which the poet triumphs

It's easy to talk about this and that;
the TV, the weather, the dog, the cat.
But what of the words that are left unsaid?
The things of which you should have talked instead?

The situations forever broken,
haunted by the ghosts of words unspoken,
and the absence of a proper exchange.
Little wonder that nothing much changes.

But imagine if you could fight that fear,
find the right words so that you can steer
tricky conversations without baulking;
if you could do that, well, now you're talking.

Brian Bilston

TESTIMONIALS

■ "The HardTalk Handbook provides a clear, focused, practical and user-friendly way to achieve better success in the difficult conversations that all of us have on a daily basis. Dawn's comprehensive approach is not overly prescriptive, but provides flexible tools for everyone to improve how they make the HardTalk easier and more profitable for both parties involved.

I've spent most of the last three decades living in different international cities outside the country of my birth, and I am sure that these lessons will have highly effective cross-cultural impact.

As such, the Handbook provides an invaluable contribution to my business and personal development, into which I expect to dip in future for handling tips on a very regular basis. I commend it highly."

Steve Harrison MVO MBE - CEO & Founding Partner, H Squared Consultants

■ "The HardTalk Handbook does an excellent job in explaining issues that most need to understand. In fact, I think this is such a good book, that I want to not only get a copy for myself but keep a few to give to people whom I think desperately need to read this to understand what is it that is stopping them from getting where they want to go. I am sure that it will be a raging success."

Mishal Kanoo – Chairman, The Kanoo Group

■ "Everyone avoids HardTalk. This can be very expensive for organisations and debilitating for all concerned. Dawn Metcalfe's HardTalk is full of great advice which is worth reading and re-reading again and again. Dawn has distilled a lot of wisdom into 170 pages and I intend to keep a copy of HardTalk in the top drawer of my desk so I will be reminded daily of really important concepts that we overlook at our cost."

Gerry Murphy - Author,
The Accidental Entrepreneur

■ "Everyone speaks. Those who get what they want are the ones who can convey their message the best. Effectively communicating what's in your mind to another person is what separates frustration from satisfaction. Dawn Metcalfe's HardTalk takes her experiences having travelled the globe, realizing even like-speaking people often are saying completely separate things with the same words and boils all of that down to simple lessons to bolster your own ability to use the right words, with the right attitude, at the right time."

Dane Rauschenberg -
Extreme Athlete - Author - Speaker

■ "Candour is key to success. Without it we don't surface problems and can't solve them. We need people to tell us what they're really thinking so we can make great decisions. But not everyone finds this easy to do. This book teaches them how to do it in a way that builds relationships. It also helps those who need to listen more effectively. I'll be buying a copy for my team for sure!

Katharine Birbalsingh – Head teacher,
Michaela Community School

■ "Dawn hits the nail on the head regarding how to gain confidence in the challenging conversations that are an important part of life. This book packs a lot of punch by being

TESTIMONIALS

pragmatic, impactful and illuminating! Thanks Dawn, from everyone who is challenged by HardTalk conversations."

Kristen Pressner - CHRO and a Top 30 Global Influencer in HR Tech of 2018

■ "As a lawyer, executive and project manager, every day I face the challenge of having difficult conversations, often surrounding disagreements. HardTalk provides many practical tools that anyone can adapt to their hard conversations. Without a doubt this is the most relevant and helpful book I've read on being more effective at HardTalk."

Paul Pelletier - Managing Director, PP Consulting

■ "In an age when organisations must achieve more with less, under-performance must be dealt with. This book will help have challenging conversations in a way that leads to a positive result. A must read for business leaders who want the best for their organisations."

Richard Nugent - Managing Director, Twenty One Leadership

■ "*Hard Talk* is more than a book; it is a manual on effective inter-personal communication. The book's solutions have a high positive impact on the effectiveness of one's overall inter-personal relationships and even how one thinks. What makes this book so effective is a focus on providing both detailed directions as well as case studies to support and build upon the core ideas and discussions. The book borrows from cognitive behavioural theory, possibly the most effective tool in psychology's toolbox, and helps train the reader to recognize the difference between emotions and thoughts. Building on this foundation there are multiple exercises that help the reader to manage, or accept, reactive emotions but act in a thoughtful, effective manner. I was pleasantly surprised to find that this is not a one or two concept book, it really covers possibly the whole breadth of inter-personal communication."

Sabah Al Binali – CEO, Universal Strategy

■ "A highly recommended read for leaders in diverse societies and organisations, Dawn's comprehensive insights, combined with her practical approach, make HardTalk an essential guide for anyone who wants to master the skill of effective intercultural communication."

Professor Martin Spraggon - Associate Dean, Mohammed Bin Rashid School of Government

■ "I understand this book was written as the reading material for the HardTalk learning & development programme, nevertheless, in its own right, I would recommend it as a must-read book for anyone who needs to have a difficult conversation, who needs to convey an unpalatable message - whether as the boss with a team member, whether it is with a team colleague or with the boss, or indeed with a friend or family member. My congratulations to Ms Metcalfe on the breadth and depth of learning she has provided in HardTalk.

Tony McVerry - Managing Director, Esquires Coffee

TESTIMONIALS

■ "There are so many great things about this book. It is full of concrete examples, which are essential to helping people to understand the topic better and learn from it. The structure from preparation to completion of the talk, along with the opportunity for readers to personalise their experience of it, is logical and appealing. The innovative way the reader can connect with the reference material and the author online via the website and social media is not only a new approach, but one that will ensure these skills 'stick'. This is a credible and essential book, not to be missed."

Danilo Cassani - MENA VP, Takeda Pharmaceuticals

■ "This is an extremely well written book with a structure and layout that will maximise understanding and retention. Perfect for professionals to improve their communication and talk about difficult subjects."

Essa Al Mulla - Deputy Director, ENDP (Emirates National Development Programme)

■ "I was delighted for the opportunity to read this book and would recommend it to anybody like myself who is a salesperson (isn't everybody?). Chapter 7 on Listening is so very important and on its own is a must read for anybody interested in developing their sales/listening skills. I will be recommending The HardTalk Handbook to all my colleagues in the Sherry FitzGerald Group."

John O'Reilly - Managing Director, Sherry FitzGerald O'Reilly, Commercial Real Estate, Naas, Ireland

■ "Any person that manages or works with others should read this book. Which one of us has not postponed the HardTalk that we know is required or indeed, avoided it altogether, because we were afraid of feeling uncomfortable or being seen by our colleagues as *"not a nice person"*. In this book Dawn Metcalfe not only explains the absolute necessity to have the conversation, but also outlines the strategies we all can use to make the having of the HardTalk of benefit to all involved with interesting case histories and practical examples. She has made a difficult subject very accessible with easy to follow work sheets, I know I will be referring back to this book many times in the future."

Steve McGettigan - Director of Marketing and Communications, Sims IVF

■ "This has to be one of the easiest "business books" to read. It's frank, honest, entertaining and sometimes makes the reader feel a little uncomfortable in places. But isn't that the point of the book and the subject matter? It sows together many best practices that we might have come across as snippets somewhere else in our lives or careers previously, and it makes no apologies. The "sound bites" of genuine scenarios bring theory to life – especially the coach's "follow up day" with the CEO. The reader might conclude that they know this stuff already, but if that was true, then why are they reading this and why weren't they putting what they thought they knew into action, and why aren't their organisations or marriages more effective? We don't all have to be FBI Agents to figure out how to listen, but having read this book, perhaps I can apply to be one now! [If that hasn't got your interest to read this book…not sure what will. You must be perfect]"

Nicholas F. Fisher - Chief Executive Officer

TESTIMONIALS

■ "I really enjoyed learning new ways to have those difficult conversations which are critical for healthy productive relationships in the workplace. I recommend this Handbook for anyone who has ever shied away from a tough conversation....which is most people on the planet."

Mark Robinson – CEO, CBI

■ "We are always told to talk....talk it over, talk it out, talk through a problem.....talking gets situations, issues and concerns in the open. However, how often do people have the initiative, confidence and security to talk in the work environment? I have been an Executive Search consultant for over 20 years and I am continuously surprised how many individuals never have those hard conversations with their managers, peers or subordinates to make their working environment more efficient and ultimately more pleasurable. When speaking to candidates of mine looking to make a move to another organisation it is more often than not due to unresolved issues with team members who disappoint. HardTalk is a straightforward talk to us all. Dawn Metcalfe has produced a step by step how-to solution to having those conversations that are needed in any organisation. It is a joy to read – its presentation, graphics and straight style of prose is refreshing and compelling. Written in clear and persuasive language, I would recommend it to anyone, at any level, to help change their outlook and hopefully their behaviour in their workplace."

Karla Dorsch - Managing Director, Piedmont Ltd

■ "The HardTalk Handbook is a very welcome addition to a society that is characterised by ever-increasing personal anxiety. Dawn Metcalfe deserves great credit for writing such a well-crafted book. It is a practical, rational and concise guide with useful tools, exercises and tips for dealing with people, understanding their behaviour and constructively speaking up. It's a useful guide not only to those in management but anyone dealing with people at any level. Dawn's approach is direct and she is clearly drawing from her own extensive travels and experiences with people of many different cultures and ethnic backgrounds. The core message is 'Treat others as THEY would like to be treated' and it certainly provides the sound advice on how to 'live' this statement."

Mark FitzGerald – Chairman, Sherry FitzGerald Group

■ "Being able to have effective HardTalk conversations is a key differentiator for senior leaders now and in the future of work. Dawn provides a practical playbook for deconstructing difficult conversations, and building the skills to move from avoidance to action."

Alison Anderson - Human Resource Director, Chartered Accountants Ireland

■ "Leading managers & their teams in Call Centre sales and customer service delivery channels in the insurance industry poses considerable daily challenges for all involved. A key challenge is one of effective leadership communication with our teams in ensuring consistency of performance, in improving performance, and most importantly, in dealing with underperformance. This excellent book by Dawn Metcalfe highlights the importance of discipline in dealing with issues, outlines the benefits of not putting-off difficult conversations, and provides

TESTIMONIALS

the knowledge & skills to carry out such conversations. It illustrates how to engender increased self-awareness & increased clarity of responsibilities - by all parties - in a HardTalk scenario, with a view to achieving commitment for a new result. 'HardTalk' will be an important part of my management toolkit from here on."

Richard Glavin – Commercial Director, Chill Insurance

■ "A fascinating and insightful read. If only the corporate world stopped to think about all that HardTalk encapsulates. Behaviour in the workplace, be it good or bad, boils down to diversity, perception, observation, reaction and emotion. Spread the word to all employers and sign them up for HardTalk; a truly brilliant piece of work that is invaluable for the professional working world - thank you!"

Sunita Singh-Dalal - Partner, AC&H LEGAL CONSULTANTS

■ "HardTalk is an erudite, entertaining take on how to converse effectively in the workplace, especially on subjects people don't want - or know how - to talk about. Presented in digestible, easy to read units, HardTalk wears its wisdom lightly and shares it generously. Its Irish born author uses her impressive cross-cultural experiences - having lived and worked in various parts of Europe, Japan, China, and UAE currently - to inform hard won insights into how to navigate and negotiate across the inevitable and mostly unspoken divides of personality, culture, values, biases, expectations. This book will be especially useful to anyone who works in a multicultural environment, which, these days, means practically everyone. It offers

good, practical advice throughout with many scenarios to illustrate its key points. The chapter on listening is especially useful, for every kind of relationship. If readers borrow the writer's empathy and good humour in dealing with people very different from themselves, they will be that much closer to getting the results they want."

Dr. Betty Sugarman - Professional Development

■ "The HardTalk Handbook speaks about the effectiveness and importance of communication in the corporate environment. Many times we may feel the urge to communicate but fail to convey our message correctly through our judgements of others. The content here is instrumental towards learning how to express ourselves in ways that others can understand and relate to. I strongly recommend all corporate professionals to read this book and, more importantly, implement the content in their routine life."

Dr. Zakir Malik - General Manager, Group HR Oasis Investment

■ "The HardTalk HandBook has a lot of great content and is very thought provoking. It provides us with clear and practical tools to help us adapt our thought process and approach to situations. I would highly recommend it to the intrigued mind on a journey of self-awareness."

Farah Foustok - Lazard

■ "In the corporate world you need to be prepared to have tough conversations to be successful. *The HardTalk Handbook* is based off 20 years of experience and in-depth research in what it takes to communicate effectively.

TESTIMONIALS

The book makes a wonderful point of first drawing the reader's mind to the reality of difficult conversations and the scenarios that call for them. It highlights the consequences of not having these conversations and how they permeate every angle of our lives, both at home and at work. More importantly, it provides insights on how to move from emotion to productive problem solving and from reaction to strategic action. HardTalk provides a step-by-step approach and involves the reader through various exercises, which allows for the application of learning in every chapter. Overall, this book is full of insights, rules and frameworks which impart the practical skill set to manage the most difficult conversations."

Hessa Al Ghurair - CBI

■ "The references are excellent and from quality sources. I like the use of case studies and examples which bring the theory to life. There are many useful insights and I really liked the concept of "feeling safe" at a meeting or with a group of people. There is lots of nice humour and you feel as reader you are being drawn into the challenge of HardTalk. A big congratulations to Dawn on a super piece of work on a subject that is particularly relevant to Irish executives."

Clive Brownlee - Executive MasterCoach (former MD, Guinness Ireland and Nigeria)

■ "If you read only one business book this year, HardTalk is your MUST read! Dawn Metcalfe is a master storyteller. She captivates her audience with her wit and intelligence. Writing about a topic that you think has been over-exposed, you immediately discover that HardTalk brings a refreshing, practical and innovative approach to effective communication. Dawn Metcalfe's HardTalk is a one-of-kind, truth be told book about everything you need to know about speaking and listening. If your business or your life is not where you want it to be, grab a copy of HardTalk and your life and career will be totally transformed."

Dr Patty Ann Tublin – CEO and Founder, Relationship Toolbox

FOREWORD

I first met Dawn Metcalfe, Founder of PDSi, on the professional networking platform, LinkedIn, on February 24, 2017. I remember our first conversation – it was about building trust. In that brief discussion I immediately recognized a unique trait in Dawn. She is a direct communicator. Not the blunt kind, but the rare kind that combines candor with compassion and curiosity.

From that day, until the present, I have enjoyed observing Dawn practice what she preaches in how she communicates with others. When she asked me to write the foreword for The HardTalk Handbook, I was both honored and elated as I share a passion for the work that has become Dawn's mission: helping people overcome both the fear and lack of skill in having difficult conversations.

As a leadership and career management coach, the number one problem I continue to see in business is unhealthy conflict. What's worse, 70 per cent of people when faced with conflict choose to avoid it.

We all know ignored problems become bigger problems that require more time and resources to solve. Your career, your team, and your organization simply cannot reach its full potential without developing the critical business and life skill of effectively engaging in difficult conversations.

Filled with engaging stories, case studies, and practical exercises, The HardTalk HandBook is the cure for the unproductive conflict ailing you, your team, and your organization's culture. Absent the straightforward and honest communication HardTalk promotes,

we are left with destructive alternatives to the truth: miscommunication, misinterpretation, and assumptions – what the HardTalk program refers to as "Potentials." Potentials are the termites of relationships and, ultimately, results.

As a former Learning & Development and Operations leader within a Fortune 20 company, I understand the importance of both developing and executing training programs that will bring a return on investment. One of the biggest drivers of ROI is learning transfer – successfully applying the behavior, knowledge, and skills acquired to the job, with a resulting improvement in performance.

Dawn's practical 4-step model is engaging, simple, and most importantly, effective. Unlike many training programs, HardTalk sticks – transferring your newly acquired knowledge and skills to the real world, where it will make all the difference for you and your teams' success.

All my best,

Kristin Sherry
Founder, Virtus Career Consulting
Author, Follow Your Star: Career Lessons I Learned from Mom &
5 Surprising Steps to Land the Job NOW!
Charlotte, N.C., U.S.A.

December 2017

CONTENTS

NOW YOU'RE TALKING 2
TESTIMONIALS 3
FOREWORD 9
PREFACE 11
INTRODUCTION 17
1. LEARN TO RESPOND, NOT REACT 27
2. CONTROL YOUR EMOTIONS 47
3. BEWARE THE PATTERN 61
4. CONSIDER THE OTHER 79
5. REMEMBER YOUR PURPOSE 87
6. BE HEARD 107
7. LISTEN 121
    ADDENDUM: A NOTE OF CAUTION 137
8. SUM IT UP 143
9. WHAT IF? 151
10. MAKE IT STICK 157
THE HANDBOOK IN SUMMARY 163
ACKNOWLEDGEMENTS 165
REFERENCES 167

PREFACE

> *"The world suffers a lot.
> Not because of the violence of bad people, but because of the silence of good people."*
>
> — Unknown

In some ways this book and the accompanying HardTalk programme are the results of more than 20 years of thinking about what it takes to communicate effectively. It is the result of my life experiences since leaving home at the age of 17.

The Ireland I grew up in was pre-Celtic Tiger, conservative and poor and so, unsurprisingly, our "immigration problem" was about how to get expatriates who left Ireland to come back home, rather than worrying about managing the intake of people from other countries. This changed over time and Ireland now seems more diverse and multicultural, more open and welcoming than I could ever have imagined growing up.

I grew up in an Ireland where it was obligatory to pass exams in Irish (sometimes wrongly referred to as Gaelic) to succeed at school or obtain many government jobs. Students who studied and sat exams in Irish received extra "points" when applying to universities and I grew up surrounded by people who only exclusively spoke one language or the other. In other words, it's no surprise that I've always been fascinated by language and the way it both brings people together and keeps them apart.

By the time I left home at 17 to move to the UK, I had lived in 19 different houses and attended four schools, albeit all in my native country, as well as spending a month doing a home-stay in Germany. At university I studied French and Spanish and was able to work in both countries for six months, negotiating my first "grown up" workplace in a third language. This also meant working out how to live with people from different cultures, with different understandings of what it meant to be "clean" or "respectful" or "hospitable". I worked with people from different generations, religions and cultures who saw the world differently and had had completely different experiences from me. I was hooked.

Living alone and working in Europe gave me the confidence to apply for the JET programme - a Japanese government-backed scheme designed to bring native English speakers into the state school system. And so, the trend continued when, on leaving University, I went to Japan, where for three years I worked in the capital city of the second most rural prefecture or state, Matsue-shi in Shimane-ken.

I arrived in Japan not speaking Japanese and having never tasted sushi or tofu (I was brought up in Ireland in the 70s and 80s!) so I pretty much fell in love right away. Even getting my dry-cleaning done or buying cockroach repellent in the supermarket became an adventure involving laughter, crying and, on occasion, a desire to commit murder or hide away in shame at my mistakes.

It all seemed very exotic (this sentiment was reciprocated it seemed, as I was regularly asked to sign autographs simply for being foreign) - nobody looked like me and the "languages" we didn't share were many. Not only did I lack basic words like "tomorrow" and "go", I couldn't even look them up because of the nature of the Japanese "alphabets". I also couldn't understand the gestures.

It was frustrating to be surrounded by a number of clearly annoyed middle-aged Japanese ladies (arms held in front of their bodies in a cross, repeating the syllables "da me") and not be able to help them. But it was great practice to realise that I needed to behave in a way that helped them to realise that my offence was caused by ignorance and not a desire to upset even if, as I worked out eventually, I had just walked on *tatami* (Japanese floor covering that shouldn't be walked on) in slippers designed only to be worn in the bathroom. This is a serious offence in Japan and was one of thousands of incidents where a presumtion of innocence has helped me get out of a tricky situation. It's an attitude I try to bring to HardTalk situations, as you'll see.

Even colours in Japan meant different things. Mustard for example, was inexplicably packaged in red and not the yellow or brown it "should" be. And I didn't know what I didn't know - I entirely lacked context and so couldn't even ask questions designed to help me avoid problems. This was made clear on my second week at work when I was late - again a serious offence in Japan. I'm a punctual person, believing five minutes early to be verging on late, and so I was truly upset when I realised I had kept my colleagues waiting and upset their plans. It took me another three days to work out that my school had a two-week timetable, with different times each week. Nobody told me because, of course, that's how schools work in Japan, and I didn't ask, because how could I have known what question would work?

To be honest it was exhausting. This was before the internet really got going and phone calls and air travel were very expensive, so it was a much more immersive experience than travelling is now.

Immersion is great for learning a language and understanding a culture but not good for rest and relaxation - I vividly remember going back to London and checking into a hotel with a feeling of absolute elation at the certainty that, no matter what was said I would understand it and be able to respond to it coherently and appropriately - the luxury of communicating in one's first language.

Despite it being exhausting, it was an amazing experience and I stayed three years, becoming proficient in Japanese before deciding to move to China to an even more remote place. In Matsue there had been only five (obvious) foreigners in a town of less than 200,000. In China, I would be the only Westerner in a town more than twice that size, and one of a handful in an enormous province of 26 million people. I was also the first female foreigner ever to live in the town, and only the third ever foreigner. I had got used to being "different" and unusual, and I wasn't scared of learning another language, but China was a different level.

Before, I had been asked for my autograph and been given awards simply for being foreign.

I had been asked to stand in front of a class and be touched by a group of schoolchildren, but the Japanese were part of the first world.

Where I lived in China, people still lived in caves - the older generation had lived through Mao and all that came after that. The only way to see anything I recognised was an overnight bus to the nearest city, many hours away. What could we possibly have in common? How could we communicate? The opportunities to mess up were immense and I did. Often.

But I learned a lot about how to get better at communicating.

I've learned to focus on what I want to achieve and what the other person needs to see and hear to perceive me and the world that way.

I've learned how our filters affect the judgements we make about what we see and hear. How they do this so quickly that we often don't even notice, making real communication very difficult, and reducing the curiosity that is at the heart of all communication.

I've learned that curiosity is key to the skill given most lip-service and yet least focus, despite it being fundamental to building knowledge and changing minds; the skill of listening.

ListeningHard is key to understanding not just the text, but also the sub-text, and can be the difference between building relationships and creating an international incident.

I've learned that you can build empathy (quickly) with just about any other human in the world and that, if you want to stay safe as a young woman travelling and living alone in remote places without friends or family nearby, you better do so.

I've learned that you can make this your life's work and still get it wrong. I've made some awful mistakes along the way - upsetting others and putting my own objectives at risk by not taking the time to think but the most important thing I've learned is this:

> *It is possible to speak up - always. There may be consequences if you do, particularly if you do it badly, but you can always do it. If you don't speak up, nothing changes.*

I've now lived in the UAE for almost 10 years and I'm privileged to live and work with people from every part of the planet. It is one of the most multi-cultural places in the world. The statistics vary but, according to the UAE government there are 200 nationalities living and working in Dubai alone, representing more than 80 per cent of the city's population. It's amazing and it should be a huge resource for the country.

I work across a lot of different industries. I can see that the "filters" that make effective communication difficult are more than just culture, gender or generation. They also include education and training, and every kind of experience that goes into making us who we are.

Diversity is a wonderful thing. Every piece of research tells us so, and we'll hear more about it later in the book, but diversity alone isn't enough: we need inclusion. In other words we need everyone "to hear and be heard".

But, ironically, diversity can make inclusion difficult, as it can make us cautious. Often too cautious. Too cautious to speak up. This is dangerous because there are consequences of *not* speaking up just as there are to speaking up.

Diversity stops us speaking up because the more your "filters" differ from others, the more difficult it is to communicate effectively. But not speaking up means bad things for individuals and teams.

In 2016 we carried out some research around a particular kind of HardTalk - bad behaviour in the workplace. Despite 90 per cent of respondents saying they had experienced this, only 30 per cent spoke up. This is not good news for things organisations care about like morale, quality and turnover, because human beings don't just see "bad behaviour" and then carry on.

No, the issue either gets resolved through a HardTalk or it festers. Instead of dealing with the subject, our research suggests people instead indulge in all kinds of behaviour that has dreadful results for them, others, and their organisation.

They avoid the topic or the person, or gossip, or even leave their job.

Clearly this has horrible consequences for morale, then quality and turnover, and ultimately the bottom line. All because people are afraid or don't want to have a difficult conversation!

We need people to speak up if they are to perform well in teams.

Google's Project Aristotle[1], conducted in 2017, identified each team member speaking more or less the same amount as being crucial to high performance. The fact that it's difficult to make that happen when working with a diversified team just makes it more likely that those who achieve it will be successful.

Of course, some people, because of their filters, will find it harder than others to either "hear" or "be heard". But everyone can get better at it if they are convinced of the need and given the tools to do so.

Everybody needs to have difficult conversations, whether it's

- *telling somebody they smell bad*
- *asking for more money*
- *convincing your colleagues to support a proposal*
- *getting your child to open up about a problem*
- *confronting a direct report about underperformance*
- *dealing with sexist or racist behaviour*

It doesn't matter where you come from, how old you are, what gender or educational background you come from, these are difficult topics. No sane person looks forward to them. But if we can master the skills of HardTalk,

we can get better at being able to achieve the purpose of having these difficult conversations - to be heard and to hear - so that we make better decisions and get better results.

We asked people why they didn't speak up when they saw bad behaviour. They told us they were afraid of retribution, or causing offence and didn't know *how* to speak up.

These kind of conversations - done well, badly, or not done at all - make a difference to relationships, to results, to happiness, to culture, to morale and to people's careers.

And we're not wired well for them.

We often seem to behave badly, just when we need to behave well! It's not that we don't know what to do. It's that we know but don't seem to be able to manage our behaviour in the moment - to learn to respond, not react, for our own sake and that of the people around us.

I wrote this book because the people I work with every day care about the following things, and HardTalk is a key skill in all of them:

1 DECISION MAKING

Simply put, if you're a knowledge worker (and you probably are if you're reading this), then it's at least part of your job to (help) make good decisions. It doesn't matter where you're working or what you're doing, we agree with the work done by Milkman, Chugh and Bazermann at Harvard[2] who say: *"In a knowledge-based economy, we propose that a knowledge worker's primary deliverable is a good decision."*

In other words, you have to speak up and be heard for the sake of your organisation, and your career. Not to mention it's what you're paid for. You've also got to get other people involved and get them to speak up, because that's how good decisions get made.

② EXECUTION

We'd go even further than our academic friends and say that making a good decision isn't enough. It's relatively easy to make a decision. Good decisions where everyone is heard are harder. Getting those decisions executed effectively and efficiently is the real test. And HardTalk is key to that. If people don't speak up, then you don't get to hear the potential problems in execution. If they don't feel listened to, and respected, how likely are they to have truly *"bought-in"*?

③ LEARNING

No matter who you are or where you are in an organisation, you don't know everything - you can't. And even if you did, as the highly regarded engineer Temple Grandin (who has autism) remarked, *"you need to have different kinds of minds working together"* to solve complex problems.

Being able to get others, particularly those different from you, to speak up and tell you how they see the world is a great leadership skill. You might be thinking "but shouldn't they just speak up?" Well, yes, maybe, but if you care about the result you'll help them, because the best ideas won't always come from the people who find it easiest to speak up.

I'm sorry to say, you also have to find a way to work with the people you don't enjoy working with, because they have strengths you don't.

④ CREATIVITY

The world is complicated and coming up with creative solutions to tough problems is key to success.

The more exposure to difference you have, the more likely you are to be creative.

It can be surprisingly difficult to get this exposure, particularly as you become more senior (and so more foreboding), or if you are different in some other way e.g. being the only man on an otherwise all-female team or the only millennial in a Gen Y office.

Think of it as a spectrum: the further to the right you go toward a closed network, the more you repeatedly hear the same ideas, which re-affirm what you already believe. The further left you go toward an open network, the more you're exposed to new ideas. If you can improve your HardTalk skills you will be, at the very least, exposed to a hugely different level of ideas compared to a person who is unable to have HardTalk.

⑤ INTEGRITY

Speaking up is usually the right thing to do. For everyone's sake.

If you're like most people, you know you should address issues, but you don't want to be the bad guy, upset your colleagues or make them angry. Too often this means we don't give people the feedback they need in the way they need it - so they can improve.

We worry too much about the negative implications for us, and not enough about all the other positive outcomes. As we'll see in a later chapter, this human tendency to care more about potential loss than potential gain is one of the "BrainDrain" factors.

⑥ ACCOUNTABILITY

Holding people - ourselves and others - accountable is how things get done. If you aspire to have any leadership abilities at all, you have to be able to hold people accountable, and not just when they report directly to you. This is a skill. Carolyn Everson, who runs global marketing for Facebook, part of an empire that includes Instagram, WhatsApp, and Oculus Rift, talks about this skill - they call it Hard Conversations - and how vital it is to managing others and the culture[3]. No matter where you are in the organisation you need to hold yourself and others accountable if you want to be considered a leader!

7 RESULTS

You've got no choice but to have HardTalk if you want great results. Tempting though it is, avoiding difficult conversations leads to less than great results.

You have to have the HardTalk if you want anything to change. The world is complex, you can't manage it alone. You need to capture the collective intelligence and get deeper, richer information. You need to get other people to speak up, and you need to do so yourself. Even if it's uncomfortable. When we don't do it we're often letting somebody down, even if it's ourselves.

Despite caring about making good, creative, implementable decisions that improve organisations and lives, many people still don't speak up. Perhaps this is because the connection between the conversation and the results isn't obvious. Surely if there were a direct link, people would get over their discomfort and speak up? And if that direct link were to a matter of life and death they definitely would, wouldn't they?

It seems not. According to research carried out in the United States by the American Association of Critical Care Nurses[4] 84 per cent of physicians reported seeing a colleague do something to put a patient's life at risk and yet only 17 per cent spoke up. If even doctors won't speak up when they see an actual life at risk, what hope is there for the rest of us?

The hope lies in the places where it does work. The hope lies in the fact that when people are given the skills, (and an opportunity to practice them with supportive leaders who don't just accept, but insist, on difficult conversations), they, and their organisations, flourish. The hope lies in the research taking place right now, and in the last 20 years, on how the brain works and what it takes to communicate effectively. The hope lies in people like you reading this and putting the tools to use.

Ideally, as we'll see, you'd have a culture and leadership team behind you. But you can do a lot as an individual, and cultures are, of course, the result of the decisions of a group of individuals. If we wait until everybody is on board then we'll never build a culture where candour is considered normal. We'll miss out on opportunities to build happiness, to create "Leaderful organisations", and to see knowledge transferred and capacity built. All of these need HardTalk: they need us to hear and be able to be heard.

HardTalk isn't just useful for the results we want to see as individuals. As you'll see throughout the book, the benefits of successful HardTalk can be transformative for teams and organisations. As demonstrated by the success of companies who have developed a culture of candour and communication, HardTalk's effectiveness can be measured in improved performance, employee retention and a better bottom line. A team that works well together will always perform better.

INTRODUCTION

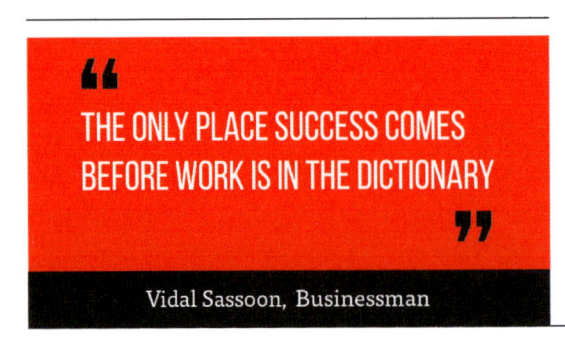

> **THE ONLY PLACE SUCCESS COMES BEFORE WORK IS IN THE DICTIONARY**
>
> Vidal Sassoon, Businessman

This book was written as the companion to the HardTalk programme, although it also works as a stand-alone guide to having the difficult conversations that make a difference to the results we get in our lives.

Designed to be read in one go and then dipped into over time, we focus primarily on workplace situations with lots of case-studies and examples to illustrate particular points and exercises to encourage you to put the skills you learn into practice. Having said that, difficult conversations or HardTalk can happen anywhere - even (especially?) in personal relationships, and the principles and skills needed are the same in any environment.

The HardTalk HandBook is deliberately named because it asks you to get involved. It's not a set of "listicles" because working with other humans, which is what difficult conversations are all about, is more nuanced than that. Instead, we present a number of principles and skills you can use at various stages of a difficult conversation - before, during and after.

Over the years we've asked hundreds of people what to do in a difficult conversation to get the results you want, and received lots of great answers. In fact, most people are very clear on what it takes - when shown video footage or told about a disastrous conversation they can identify what went wrong, and give great advice on how to make it better. And yet these same people readily admit to not following their own advice when it's important.

What's going on? How can we know what to do, believe it is important to do, and still not do it when it matters most? The answer is that the "weakest link" in any HardTalk scenario is ourselves. Managing our own behaviour in moments of stress (clearly part of any difficult conversation) - remembering to do these things - to do what you know is the right thing - is the most difficult part of any HardTalk.

We help with this by looking at the *"BrainDrains"* or ways our neurobiology works against us; and the *"BrainTrains"*, our tools and strategies to manage the BrainDrains.

INTRODUCTION

BrainDrains™
Some ways your brain makes HardTalk harder

BrainTrains™
Some tools and strategies to fight the BrainDrains

This book will not just explain what to do in HardTalk scenarios, and why it works. It also covers why it's so hard to do (the BrainDrains) and gives you tips and advice on what you can do to fix that (the BrainTrains).

This focus on ourselves is Phase 1 of the HardTalk model, WorkHard.

01 WorkHard™

WorkHard™ - the hard, cognitive work that needs to be done before we speak up including using the HardTalk DecisionTree and an Agile Learner approach

Throughout the book, there are many examples, case studies and opportunities to get more involved through quizzes and, via the blog, reading research.

The exercises are as realistic as we can make them, with scenarios and case-studies either based on real-life experience or as an amalgam of a number of different situations we've observed or heard about as trainers, facilitators and coaches over the years.

The advice is practical, and we've seen it work. We don't promise to make every conversation easy and make every annoying colleague/scary competitor/difficult boss disappear, but if you practice the skills presented here *(see Chapter 10 for how to "Make it Stick")* and get useful feedback, you will climb the Ladder of Learning and get better!

Ladder of Learning

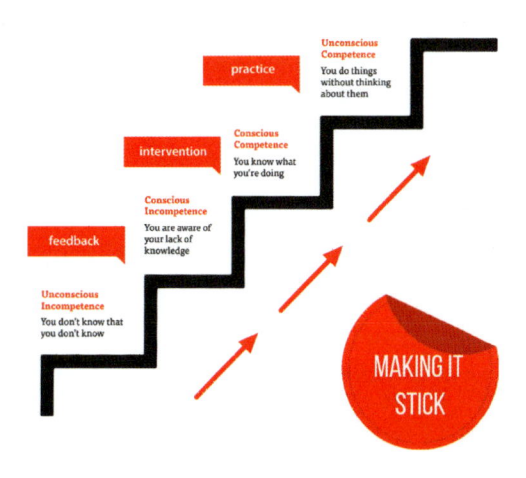

Unconscious Incompetence — You don't know that you don't know
feedback
Conscious Incompetence — You are aware of your lack of knowledge
intervention
Conscious Competence — You know what you're doing
practice
Unconscious Competence — You do things without thinking about them

MAKING IT STICK

18

As with any set of new skills you are most likely to perfect them if you practice, and you are most likely to practice if you see the relevance. For that reason please do think of examples from your own life when reading the book, and challenge yourself to do the work of answering the questions posed.

Reading the case studies gives a broader sense of how the skills might work in practice, but it's only by applying them to your own life that you will see a difference.

If you are struggling to think of a HardTalk scenario you're currently avoiding, or any that didn't go as well as you had hoped, then congratulations - you probably don't need to waste any more time on this book.

Some generic examples include situations where you need to:

- Give someone else bad news
- Negotiate effectively
- Convince others to speak up
- Make good decisions
- Get decisions implemented
- Get and give effective feedback
- Build a culture of openness, creativity and innovation
- Build a happy place to work
- Confront someone about performance or behaviour that needs to be changed (such as favouritism, lack of setting an example, or discrimination)
- Deal with behaviour affecting team morale or effectiveness (for example, a lack of awareness of how a behaviour is perceived negatively by others)

Whatever the topic (and as we'll see in Chapter 1 choosing the topic isn't as easy as it might at first seem!) our simple four-phase model is presented to help readers prepare for and communicate effectively during their own HardTalk scenarios.

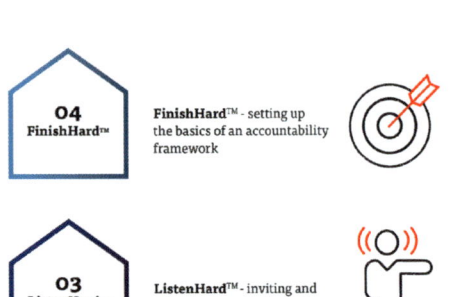

04 FinishHard™ - setting up the basics of an accountability framework

03 ListenHard™ - inviting and reflecting to get to the truth

02 SpeakSoft™ - declaring and explaining in a way that minimises defensiveness and shows your best motives

01 WorkHard™ - the hard, cognitive work that needs to be done before we speak up including using the HardTalk DecisionTree and an Agile Learner approach

The first phase, as we can see, is WorkHard, which is all about the cognitive work you need to do before you ever open your mouth or engage with another person in a HardTalk scenario.

In this phase, we look at what makes HardTalk hard and what is happening in our brain to stop us from speaking up, or to convince us to behave in a way that we know is not in our best interest. We then consider tools we can use to help us manage our emotions, and so our behaviour. We finish off thinking about ourselves by looking at how we can work against our brain's tendency to be lazy and succumb to patterns.

INTRODUCTION

> **HardTalk partner: the person with whom you're having the conversation**

Our focus then turns to the other person or persons in the conversation - throughout the book we've used one or maybe two HardTalk partners in the scenarios. Of course, the principles are the same when working with groups - and how to make sure they see us how we need them to see us.

In Chapter 6, we return to our behaviour as we think about Phase 2 and what it means to SpeakSoft or in a way that minimises defensiveness, and allows us to talk about almost anything with almost anyone.

Staying with our behaviour, Chapter 7 moves us to Phase 3, where we appeal to our basest instincts and learn the need to ListenHard for our own sake as well as those around us.

We conclude by looking at how to finish a HardTalk in a way that makes life easier and more productive and try to answer some of the Frequently Asked Questions we get when we talk to students of HardTalk. We also give you some advice and resources you can use to continue learning about and practising HardTalk so that the skills become part of the repertoire you use every day.

A number of themes permeate the book and might be worthwhile looking at explicitly here.

1 **Use the Platinum Rule - not the Golden Rule**

The Golden Rule is "Treat others as you would want to be treated", and this is pretty good advice if the person you're dealing with is just like you. Mostly, however, the people with whom we have to interact do not have the good taste to see the world just like us. In fact, if they did we wouldn't need to have any difficult conversations at all.

If we want to influence others, then we need to see the world through their eyes: we need to think about filters - our own and theirs - and the impact these have on what we see, hear, say and do, and what we think of what others say and do. This theme is so important that it is part of every aspect of HardTalk, and so will be covered in much more detail further on.

Platinum Rule:

Treat others as THEY would want to be treated

2 **There are consequences no matter what you do**

The second major theme of HardTalk is connected to our *"Rules of Adulting"* and tells us that we can make any decision we like, but we have to live with the consequences.

Rules of Adulting

1# **The first rule is**
"You can make any decision you like but you must live with the consequences."

2# **The second rule is**
"Every action is a decision."

20

When people fail to communicate effectively there are consequences. Whether we fail to have HardTalk at all or fail to have it well (or rather whether people stay quiet or whether they speak out inappropriately) there are consequences for:

- Individuals
- Teams
- Relationships (both personal and professional)
- Organisations
- Projects

amongst others.

For example:

- Issues fester and grow and relationships suffer
- People take offence and relationships suffer
- Less good decisions get made
- Bad behaviour goes unchecked
- People don't improve
- Decisions don't get implemented
- Performance and revenue is affected

We'd go so far to say that a very large percentage of the problems in our business lives (and maybe even our personal lives) could be solved if we could only communicate effectively - if we could, as the HardTalk motto says, *"hear and be heard"*.

It's fair to say that speaking up doesn't magically change everything for the better, but it's also true that if you (or someone else) don't speak up, nothing changes.

Deciding not to have HardTalk is okay, but it means you are deciding to live with the status quo and you should, therefore, truly accept it.

If you can't - if your boss' micromanaging really does eat away at you, or your spouse's unwillingness to communicate drives you truly crazy, and you can't "let it go", then you need to have the HardTalk.

You don't get to be a bore. You don't have to speak up about everything, but you need to make a conscious choice and, if you decide to do so, you do have to do it carefully. But that is the premise behind HardTalk: most of the time, it's better to speak up and to do so effectively.

Organisations also have a responsibility to improve people's ability to speak up, especially given the impact on both morale (and so well-being), and on the bottom line.

If you don't speak up, you must let it go. Letting it go is harder than it seems and throughout the book, we will be using elements of the *DecisionTree* and the HardTalk model to avoid the pitfalls.

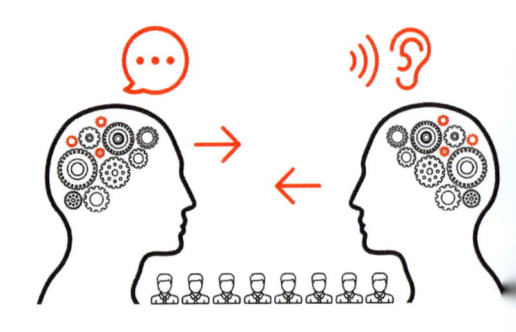

HardTalk
To hear and be heard

INTRODUCTION

DecisionTree

*(downloadable from **www.hardtalk.info**)*

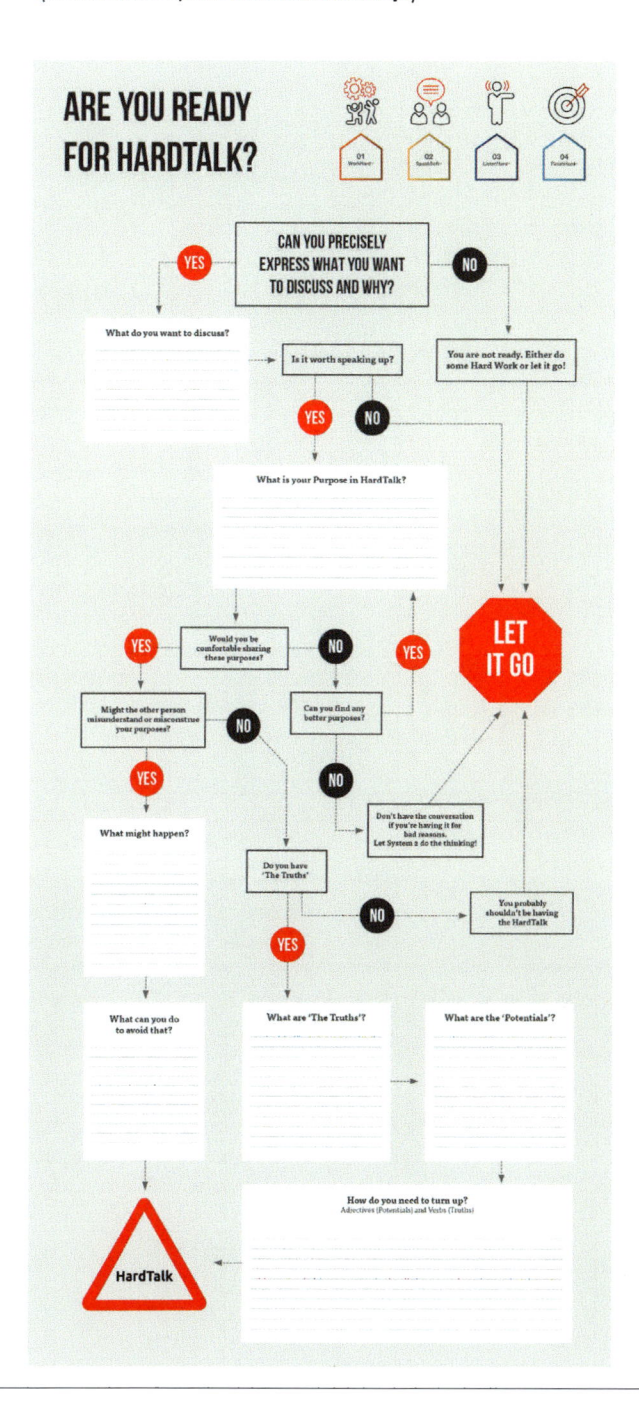

3. Curiosity is a secret weapon

How many of your day to day problems would go away if you felt they'd been heard? How much more could you learn if you could get others to trust you and to speak up? The third theme you will see throughout the book is the need to be curious about other people - not because it's a nice thing to do, (although it is), but because it will help you get the results you want.

We'd argue it's always important to be able to hear others - to make sure others speak up so that you can learn, make better decisions and spot any problems. If for example:

- you're in a phase of high growth
- in recession
- in times of stress
- when there's been a change
- in uncertainty
- when something has gone wrong
- when something might go wrong
- when trust has been broken

Then HardTalk might be even more important. These are just the times our neurobiology works against us. In these situations we know we should listen, but instead, we talk.

I know. You know how to listen. You do it every day. And anyway you agree it's important. You've been on the course. You read the book. You'll try harder. Honest! Okay.

But let me try to prove to you why it's so important. What is most at stake in your HardTalk scenarios? It's almost certainly not death - yours or other people's. But for some people it is, and they are very clear on what the key to success is. **It's listening.** And they are crystal clear on what you can do to get better at it. Because they teach it.

The FBI explicitly teach negotiators listening skills - because if you want to change someone's behaviour you need to understand it. To do that you need to listen. Curiosity, not the ability to shoot a gun, is what is most likely to create successful negotiation.

4. Take responsibility

Throughout the book, and the HardTalk programme, we have tried to be very practical and to *"show our workings"* by being clear about the research we've used and the experiences we've had in real life. Please be sceptical when anyone tells you "the research says..." There are different kinds of research and, often through the proper scientific method, our understanding changes over time. We work hard to keep our research up-to-date and we urge you to join the HardTalk community so you can keep abreast of new developments, as well as ask questions about anything to do with what you learn here.

We also want to make it clear (as we do as coaches and trainers) that the responsibility for having great HardTalk is yours.

We've provided resources throughout the HandBook and there are more available at ***www.hardtalk.info*** including customisable feedback sheets just like we use during the HardTalk training programme, so you can get useful feedback and improve over time.

Finally, we want to address the question that always comes up when we talk about HardTalk and that is: What about culture? For the purposes of answering this question, we're going to look at culture in two ways - national and organisational.

❶ National Culture

Perhaps because of where we're based - Dubai - the question of national culture and its importance to one's ability to have HardTalk successfully comes up regularly. One question we're often asked is "Does HardTalk work across all cultures?" and the answer is an emphatic yes. This doesn't mean that some people find it easier than others. This is a result of all their filters - including cultures.

We should also remember that any given culture will have some aspects that make HardTalk easier, and others that make it more challenging.

None of the behaviours essential to HardTalk success is inherently difficult - (ask for permission, start with the Truths, look for more data, paraphrase) - these and all of the other HardTalk tools are relatively easy to master. The difficulty comes in mastering them when you're under pressure, as is the case in any kind of HardTalk scenario. And that's why we spend so much time in the WorkHard phase: getting our own brains ready for HardTalk!

A big part of that process of getting our brains ready is our ability to delay gratification now for a bigger reward later. You may already know about the Marshmallow Test.[5]

In 1972 researchers told a series of children if they could spend about 15 minutes alone in a room without eating a tempting marshmallow they would be given a reward - an extra marshmallow. As it turns out, it wasn't just an amusing experiment to see how much self-control kids have when faced with confectionery. The kids were tracked over time and it turned out that those who could delay gratification ended up with higher SAT scores, lower levels of substance abuse, lower likelihood of obesity, better responses to stress, better social skills as reported by their parents, and generally better scores in a range of other life measures.

We know willpower and determination are connected to the ability to stay focused on long-term results rather than short-term pleasure - to delay gratification. We also know

"We must all suffer from one of two pains: the pain of discipline or the pain of regret. The difference is discipline weighs ounces while regret weighs tonnes."
— Jim Rohn[6], Entrepreneur

the ability to deny ourselves in the short-term has a long-term impact on more than just how many marshmallows we get to eat!

This is important to HardTalk because success usually comes down to choosing the pain of discipline in the moment, to get the results you want in the long run. That's exactly what delayed gratification is all about.

Cameroon is a society where some aspects of the culture - a deference to hierarchy, for example, might make HardTalk more difficult as it's harder to speak up against seniority (and harder to listen when you're senior!). But when the Marshmallow Test was conducted there (for the first time outside of Europe) it turns out Cameroonian kids do better.
Much better.

Some 70 per cent of kids in Cameroon were able to wait for their treat versus only 30 per cent in Germany. The researchers speculate it's the deference to hierarchy - the children are used to being told what to do, and the expectation is that they will do it.

HardTalk is complicated. There isn't a set of rules. It's about self-awareness and self-control. It's a process.

❷ Organisational culture

Perhaps counter-intuitively, our experience suggests organisational culture might be even more important than national culture. Again, this might be because of the "mixed salad" that is our home territory, a place where workplace culture can supersede individual national cultures.

There are great opportunities to build a culture where HardTalk is valued; where the skills that underlie important activities and objectives like happiness, knowledge transfer and capacity building, are nurtured, and individual employees and teams are expected to hear and be heard. It also means, as we'll see, that without strong leadership, a HardTalk culture is unlikely to develop.

Another group of scientists recently replicated the Marshmallow Test but with a difference.[7] Before giving the children a marshmallow and offering to double it if they waited, the researchers split them into two groups. The first group was exposed to inconsistency (they were made promises that weren't fulfilled). The second group, on the other hand, got exactly what they were promised: they were exposed to consistency.

What do you think happened? Perhaps unsurprisingly, the children who had been trained to see delayed gratification as a good thing (the second group) waited an average four times longer than the first group.

Organisations and their leaders should be aware of the importance of consistency in HardTalk, as in so many other areas. Saying you have a culture isn't enough, it must be seen in every behaviour of every employee, at all levels of the organisation.

Throughout the book we often use successful organisations as evidence of the potential of HardTalk and to provide 'real world' examples of it in action. Many you will recognise, such as Facebook and Google, but one you might not, is the Michaela Community School in London. Founded by Katharine Birbalsingh in 2014, the school has a formidable reputation and a distinctive outlook approach to achieving success. Their motto 'Knowledge is Power' is reflected in the school's own use of the HardTalk principles which have proved invaluable in how the staff communicate amongst themselves and how they teach the children about responsibility and valuable behaviour. They were recently awarded an 'Outstanding' (the highest grade) by Ofsted, the official educational standards department of the UK Government. They are a good example of the power of HardTalk and its potential to benefit any type of work place, if it is truly part of the culture.

We work with organisations to make sure their cultures support HardTalk - or at least don't make it impossible. But what can you do if your organisation doesn't support HardTalk? Is it worthwhile even trying?

Ideally, you'd have a culture behind you, but you can do a lot as an individual, and cultures are the results of decisions made by a group of individuals. You can make change. It might take time and it might be hard but if not you, then who? If not now, then when?

We are not promising by the time you've finished this book that you will be able to walk into any situation, click your fingers and have perfect trust and empathy. What we *do* promise is that the tools and techniques we present here are based on the best available research and our observations of what works.

Being able to communicate effectively is the "secret sauce" of leadership at all levels. We've learned a lot during the last 20 years about how to get it right. So, let's get going...

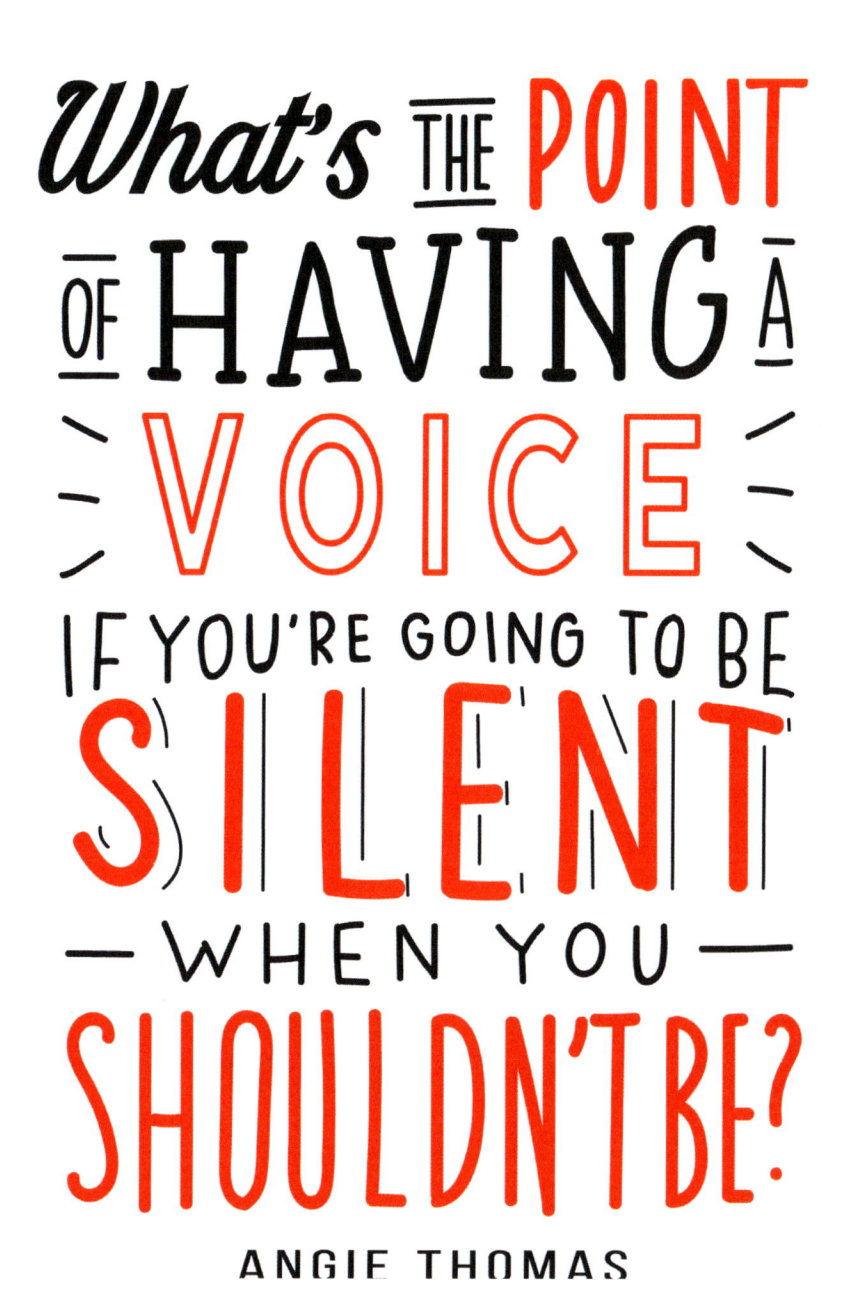

> What's the point of having a voice if you're going to be silent when you shouldn't be?
>
> — ANGIE THOMAS

LEARN TO RESPOND, NOT REACT

CHAPTER 1

Natural instincts aren't always a friend to us. In HardTalk they often work directly against our own interests. Understanding our gut reactions better will guide us to determine when we should speak up and when we should let it go.

> **FOR THERE IS NOTHING EITHER GOOD OR BAD, BUT THINKING MAKES IT SO**
>
> Shakespeare, Hamlet, Act 2, Scene 2

OUR NEUROBIOLOGY WORKS AGAINST US

Most people are "nice". There may be things we see that don't seem right, or maybe there are issues we'd like to raise, but we don't want to be the bad guy, upset our colleagues or make them angry.

So we don't speak up.

Most people are risk averse too, as we'll see later. Given the choice between the status quo and the risk of losing something, we don't think rationally. We imagine the very worst case scenario, and we imagine it as much more likely than it is.

So we don't speak up.

Most people don't like being uncomfortable.

HardTalk is, by its very nature, likely to make us feel less than comfortable as we move out of the zone where we pretend all is well, putting up with the world as it is, (while continuing to inwardly complain and waste energy), towards a zone where we take responsibility for our choices.

So we don't speak up.

These three statements hold true for all normal human beings. If you're a psychopath, you don't feel discomfort or consider the feelings of others, and you're certainly not interested in

CHAPTER 1 | 10
LEARN TO RESPOND, NOT REACT

listening, so HardTalk is probably not for you.

For all other humans – the majority - it's normal not to relish HardTalk.

There are some things than can make HardTalk even harder. For example, if:

YOU come from a culture where it is not usual to talk about the *bad stuff*

YOU work in an organization with many different cultures and are wary of causing offence

YOU are more junior or younger than the person with whom you should be having the conversation

YOU are friends with the person you feel you need to talk to

YOUR potential HardTalk partner has a track record and reputation for being *difficult* -

then you might find it more difficult to have HardTalk.

All these circumstances - and many more - may make HardTalk harder, but they don't let us off the hook. They don't mean we get to just shrug our shoulders and say *"there's nothing I can do"*. Not if we care about results.

Because, tempting though it is, avoiding difficult conversations leads to less than great results.

By handling these situations well, in a respectful way that allows the other person to hear you, process the information and work with you to come up with solutions, you can:

HELP create a culture where honest feedback happens

MANAGE conflict

ADDRESS performance issues

DEAL with small problems before they become big

We know whether it's in the boardroom, office, factory floor or hospital, results depend on our ability to work and communicate effectively with others. If you can't talk honestly with almost anybody about almost anything, you can expect poor results.

We know this.

It makes sense.

And yet we still don't do it well.

This isn't our fault. Faced with HardTalk, our brains don't react as we'd like them to, and so we have to WorkHard to counter this, starting with deciding whether or not to even speak up, and what to speak about.

01 WorkHard™

WorkHard™ - the hard, cognitive work that needs to be done before we speak up including using the HardTalk DecisionTree and an Agile Learner approach

WORKHARD 28

Difficult conversations are, well, difficult. Asking for a raise, persuading somebody that your idea is right and/or theirs is wrong, giving bad news to a supplier or direct report- nobody in their right mind enjoys these situations.

But they shouldn't be as difficult as they are, because, in fact, we all know what the "right" thing to do is and, if asked in advance how we should behave in a difficult conversation, we'd probably get it right. When we are asked to observe others either in real life or on a video in a training environment, we can tell them what they've done right and wrong. But, in the moment, we don't always do it. This isn't entirely our fault or, at least, it's the fault of our ancestors and the way their brains evolved to deal with the world.

There's a little part of our brain called the *amygdala*, and this tiny thing is very important, because when it perceives a threat to our safety, it releases *cortisol* and *catecholamines*. When these chemicals flood the brain, it stimulates the primitive limbic brain - our *lizard* or *monkey* brain - so that we can react by either running away or fighting back (the flight or fight response). This is terribly helpful if you're faced with an angry lion, but not great if it's a colleague whose underperformance you need to address, or a boss who you believe is making an uninformed decision.

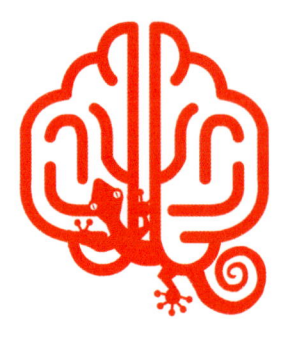

> **When the ancient limbic brain is activated, it closes down our prefrontal cortex**

When the ancient limbic brain is activated, it closes down our prefrontal cortex. And this is important because the much more recently developed prefrontal cortex is sometimes called the *executive brain* (where executive means *having the power to put plans, actions, or laws into effect.*) This is what powers creative thinking, good judgment and empathy. It is what we tend to think of when we say the word *brain*.[8]

So when we are faced with a difficult conversation, it's a neurochemical reality that it's harder to behave well. We lose bandwidth in the higher functioning areas of our brains if we feel fear or distrust, and so our ability to think and behave rationally is really compromised.

Of course, this is also true for other people in the conversation too. If your HardTalk partner doesn't trust you, they can't hear your message. If, for example, your direct report is afraid of you or your colleague doesn't believe you're on the right side, they won't be able to empathize with your agenda, or access their own *executive brain*. Quite literally, nervous people can't think straight or fully contribute. Those leaders who are proud of being *respected or feared rather than liked* might want to think about the implications of this on the performance of those around them, as making others fearful or nervous is rarely a productive or efficient approach, long term.

If difficult conversations take place in a space where our limbic brain has been turned off and our executive brain has been turned on, then we are far more likely to be able to come up with solutions and to express these solutions well. We are also more likely to be open to new ideas, to be creative, and to be innovative.

In the next Chapter we'll look at how to deal with this legacy problem of managing our emotions to make sure we behave in a way that reflects what we want, but for now I want to start by looking at the biggest problem we see in HardTalk - it's absence.

Our neurobiology works against us before as well as during a HardTalk scenario. As we approach a difficult conversation we are likely to feel all kinds of emotions and few of them will be positive - anxiety, fear, dread, nervousness - this is what we hear from people at workshops. This leads to things happening in our brains - our amygdala lighting up and our deciding to *fly*.

Most people will tell you they know what to do in a HardTalk scenario and they know that nothing changes if they don't speak up. But they don't speak up in that moment. And it's because they've allowed that *flight* reaction to render them *speechless*.

Of course, sometimes that's OK. You don't have to talk about everything. In fact, you absolutely shouldn't talk about everything.

We don't live in a world of ice-cream and baby chickens and all things lovely - there will be situations where the right thing to do is to stay quiet; yet experience suggests that, in fact, the number of times where you could speak up with some hope of success is probably larger than you think.

Of course you get to decide - you're an adult - and we're going to give you some tips and tools below to make sure you're making the right decision and not just letting the BrainDrains win. Do you remember the *Rules of Adulting*?

Over the years we've developed the 2 Rules of Adulting. The first rule is *you can make any decision you like but you must live with the consequences* and the second rule is *every action is a decision*.

In essence, this means that you can always decide to speak up or not, but you have to live with the consequences. It further says that whenever you do or don't do something that's a decision that is being made.

Later in this chapter we'll work through a number of exercises decided to help you avoid the default *flight* option and really make a decision about whether or not you should speak up. First, though, why is HardTalk so hard?

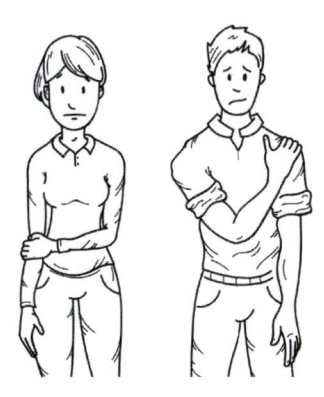

> *Speechless — staying quiet when you have something that should be heard*

HARDTALK IS HARD BECAUSE OF THREE ELEMENTS

Difference / Topic / HardTalk / Purpose

1. DIFFERENCE

Beyond our neurobiology, one of the things that makes HardTalk even harder is also something that we know is good: difference.

Think of any potential HardTalk scenario (have a look at page 19 in the introduction for some inspiration).

Imagine, first, that you were having that conversation with somebody your age and from a similar background, somebody brought up in the same religion as you, with the same socio-economic background, who speaks the same language, understands the same references, means the same thing you do when they use a word. Even in that circumstance it's still hard to tell somebody bad news or hold them accountable or say no.

Now imagine having the conversation with someone who sees the world entirely differently. It's going to be even harder.

Difference, or diversity, is good for innovation and creativity. In fact diversity is pivotal to innovation and creativity and has positive impacts on the bottom line. But it can make HardTalk harder.

Diversity can make things harder because we see the world differently and that makes it harder to communicate effectively. But how can that be? There is an abundance of research telling us diversity is good but actually diversity is pointless unless there is inclusion - unless the group and individuals in the group behave in certain ways i.e. when they build trust and speak up at about the same amount.

For now we want to look at how diversity can make conversations harder. We are all different in many ways. We all see the world through different filters - Gender, Race, Nationality, Education, Work Experience, Language, Generation, Life-phase etc.. We are all made up of lots of different things - and these different elements, like in a kaleidoscope, come together in an infinite variety of shapes and colours and this is great.

> *All of us see the world through various filters*

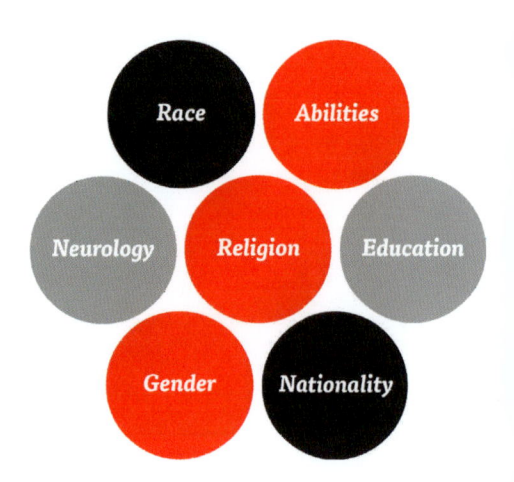

Race / Abilities / Neurology / Religion / Education / Gender / Nationality

CHAPTER 1 | 10
LEARN TO RESPOND, NOT REACT

They all lead to us thinking and behaving differently, which means we all have different strengths and weaknesses. The key is to understand this and work with it - not pretend it's not happening.

So all of us see the world through various filters. Because of where we were born, how we were taught we see the world differently. It's not right or wrong - it's what makes sense for us and to us. And, of course, what makes sense for *them* i.e. your HardTalk partner and to them. It can be quite disconcerting sometimes - do you remember the first time you stayed away from home at a friend's house and you realised that they do everything *wrong* or, rather *differently*?

Because the filters are always there we often forget about them and assume other people see the world as we do. That can lead to some nasty consequences. If you can remember that the other person is behaving in a way that makes sense to them and focus on trying to understand that, you will, as we'll see in the ListenHard chapter, go a long way to being a success at HardTalk.

There are literally dozens of different *filters* and, of course, there's no way you're going to understand another human being perfectly. But talking about filters, as well as acknowledging your own, is a great way to start.

Exercise:
How do you access information?

One way our filters differ is in how we like to access and deal with information. We often use this exercise with teams who are just starting to think about working together more effectively as it's pretty low-risk, it's not personal and allows people to share as much or as little as they like.

First, choose your usual area of focus.
Then match that to whether you tend to consider the big-picture view or the details.

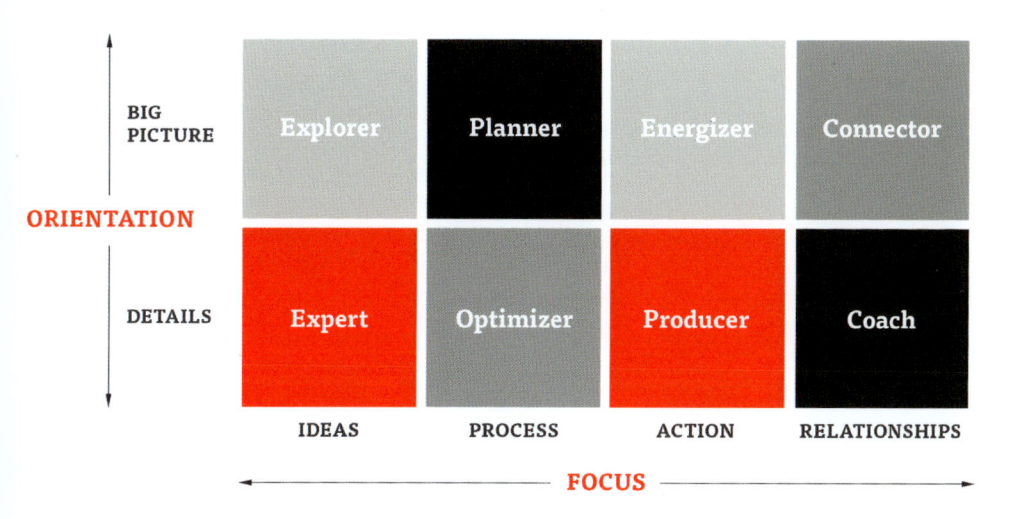

ORIENTATION	IDEAS	PROCESS	ACTION	RELATIONSHIPS
BIG PICTURE	Explorer	Planner	Energizer	Connector
DETAILS	Expert	Optimizer	Producer	Coach

FOCUS

WORKHARD 32

This exercise is about processing information - different filters might lead us to process information differently, for example, home culture.

If you're Japanese, you are more likely to want detail - and insist on this - before making a decision.

People from Arab cultures often take a leap before getting into the nitty-gritty.

The language you speak may have an impact, as will your education, your training, and who knows what else!

In this exercise, you're asked to think about what is important to you / what you enjoy doing and try to identify the category that best describes you.

You then place your colleagues on the grid using your best guess, based on your knowledge and experience of working with those colleagues.

Each individual then shares with the rest of the team where they placed themselves and why and is told where they were placed by the rest of the team members (anonymously in some cases). Any discrepancies are noted, the individual's preferences noted and any behavioural changes agreed and noted.

We can so easily bridge most of the divides between us if we try - we have much more in common than we have separating us. Acknowledging out loud, often and in advance that there are differences makes these easier to talk about and the downsides easier to avoid. But if we don't remember why other people are different - if we don't remember we all have filters and their filters are different from ours - we can find them frustrating and that is not a healthy emotion when we're going into a HardTalk scenario.

Diversity has the power to be a great asset to business but that will only happen if individuals and organisations work to make

> *We can so easily bridge most of the divides between us if we try — we have much more in common than we have separating us*

sure it does. Here are some things you can do to improve your "diversity intelligence".

❶ Travel

See for yourself how sensible, good-hearted, well-meaning people all over the world approach similar problems in very different ways but often for very sensible reasons - at least from their point of view.

❷ Read fiction

Neuroscientists mapping the brain have discovered that reading fiction taps into the same brain networks as real life experience. When you are engaged in reading a fictional story your brain is literally living vicariously through the characters at a neurobiological level. Researchers at Carnegie Mellon University have found that reading a chapter of *Harry Potter and the Sorcerer's Stone* lights up the same brain regions that would be involved in watching someone moving - or flying on a broom - in the real world.[9]

This is called the ideometer effect and refers to the fact that our thoughts can make us feel real emotions. This is why actors can use their memory or their imagination to make themselves cry or laugh convincingly on cue and why reminding yourself what you're grateful for makes you feel better.

❸ Learn a language

Bilingual children were better than monolingual children at a task that involved being able to imagine being in someone else's shoes or, put another way, at being able to think across differences. If you think about it, this makes intuitive sense. Correctly interpreting what someone else says often requires not just paying attention to what they say i.e. its content, but also to the surrounding context. What does a speaker know or not know? What did he intend to convey? Children who grow up in multilingual environments have social experiences that provide routine practice in considering the perspectives of others: they have to think about who speaks which language to whom, who understands which content, and the times and places in which different languages are spoken.

In essence, children who speak other languages are more in tune with others.

I've also personally found that learning new languages gave me an insight into the culture and so the way of thinking of those speaking the language. If a word only exists in one language that must give us some insight into the people who came up with it.

> *Cultivating curiosity requires more than having a brief chat about the weather*

❹ Ask questions

Curiosity expands our empathy when we talk to people outside our usual social circle, and discover lives and world-views very different from our own. Curiosity is good for us too: happiness guru Martin Seligman identifies it as a key strength that can enhance life satisfaction.[10]

Cultivating curiosity requires more than having a brief chat about the weather. Crucially, it is about genuinely being interested in the other person and is a key principle in HardTalk - in trying to understand the world inside the head of the other person. We'll come back to this when we learn to ListenHard.

❷ TOPIC

The second element that can make HardTalk harder is the topic. Some topics are simply *harder* than others.

These are some of the hardest topics to broach in the workplace:

WHAT KINDS OF TOPICS ARE DIFFICULT TO TALK ABOUT?

- *Inappropriate workplace attire*
- *Poor social habits - nose picking, hand gestures, table manners*
- *Using the phone too much/for too long for personal calls*
- *Using the internet inappropriately*
- *No promotion/disciplinary/ termination*
- *Repeated lateness to work or coming back from breaks*
- *Workplace romances*
- *Using phones during a meeting*
- *Gossiping*
- *Poor personal hygiene*

Of course, culture plays a role here, as do some other filters. For example, talking about somebody's weight is considered pretty much taboo in the workplace in the UK.

This wasn't the case when I worked in China or Japan where I would be told, admiringly, that I had got "got smart" when I looked trim, and heads would shake when I returned, full of my mother's home cooking, after the holidays!

In much of the West, it would seem rude to simply ask a stranger what their skin problem was. Sadly, that wasn't my experience a couple of years back in Sri Lanka when pretty much everyone just pointed and said: *Eurgh, what's that?* as they noticed my psoriasis.

Given I was suffering from an outbreak of both psoriasis and psoriatic arthritis, I was itchy, in pain, embarrassed and worried, and I'm afraid I didn't do a great job of having HardTalk.

WHAT TOPICS ARE HARD FOR YOU?

- *What kind of subjects are hard to talk about for you? Think about the times when you didn't bring up a topic or were surprised/shocked when someone else did.*

- *Generally speaking topics that are close to our heart (or that of our HardTalk partner) in some way are more likely to be HardTalk. These topics are harder because there's more emotion involved.*

- *Later we'll learn how to take out the emotion and talk about almost anything by sticking with the 'Truths' and watching out for the 'Potentials'*

③ PURPOSE

Most of us have good, healthy, purposes most of the time. We want good things for ourselves, for our colleagues, for our teams, for our organisations, for our suppliers, for our clients and we'd be prepared to share these. But many times, when we enter a HardTalk, that purpose slips away. We forget about the long-term results we want and, instead, we focus on what feels good in the short-term. And what feels good in the short-term is probably not the purpose we want other people to see us have.

> *The only way people can tell your purpose is by what you tell them — in word and deed*

In that moment our good, long-term purpose - the one we'd be happy to tell people about - slips away and the short-term purpose that we're not so proud of kicks in.

Maybe we move from wanting to understand and fix a problem to wanting to prove ourselves right or to blame our HardTalk partner. Whether we know it or not, our purpose has changed and our behaviour has changed too. The problem is that the other person can only see our behaviour and will use this to come to their own conclusions about our true purpose. This, of course, has implications for your relationship and for future HardTalk scenarios

These three elements together mean that difficult conversations are not easy to get better at. Because we're stressed, and we're thinking short-term, our neurobiology works against us. WorkingHard means learning why we tend to *misbehave* and work against our own interests in HardTalk scenarios. The next few chapters are focused on that. But before

CHAPTER 1 | 10
LEARN TO RESPOND, NOT REACT

we do anything else we need to decide what we want to talk about and whether we want to speak up at all.

Exercise:
Choose your HardTalk scenario

Below, write your HardTalk scenario. Imagine you were guaranteed to speak eloquently and persuasively. If you knew you would effectively communicate and get the results you want who would you talk to about what?

_____
_____
_____
_____
_____
_____
_____
_____
_____
_____
_____
_____
_____
_____
_____
_____
_____
_____
_____
_____
_____
_____
_____
_____

Are you sure about your HardTalk scenario? *Circle Y for Yes and N for No.*

Do you really care about the topic? **Y/N**

Is the other party involved important to you? **Y/N**

Do you really care about the result? **Y/N**

Will the issue at hand continue to bother you if you don't have the HardTalk? **Y/N**

Can you imagine losing it, one day, if the issue isn't resolved? **Y/N**

The more Ys you have the more likely you are sufficiently emotionally invested to consider, under some circumstances, having the conversation.

Exercise:
Decide on your topic

At first glance, this seems like an easy question. But, as we'll see, it's not always obvious. Imagine the following scenario...

Alba is Marketing Manager for a mid-sized family firm based in Abu Dhabi, but covering the region. She's a friend of the owner's daughter, and, as such, has unusual access to the decision makers and reports directly to the Board. Her remit is to transform the way the consumer electronics side of the business markets itself. In the six months she's been in the position, she's made a lot of changes.

In a recent meeting of the executive team, the CFO and Head of Procurement seemed to be working together to undermine Alba's proposed strategic marketing plan for the next five years, noting that it involved an increase of 30 per cent in the marketing budget, at a time when other parts of the group are facing cutbacks. The CEO seemed to back their point of view and refused to agree to support her plan at the next board meeting.

WORKHARD 36

Alba was surprised to get such pushback as she had met with each of the stakeholders to explain her plans and ask for input. She knew she had explained why a more segmented approach to the market with updated marketing collateral would cost more in the short-term but lead to greater savings further down the line. She was furious when she considered how much time she had spent in meetings with the CFO, and how she had supported him in a recent controversial decision about divesting a business of great sentimental value to the current owner of the firm.

On reflection, Alba remembered that she had heard stories in the past about the CFO and his lack of loyalty, and is concerned that he will stop her from achieving the objectives set for her by the board.

If you were Alba what would you want to discuss and with whom?

_____
_____
_____
_____
_____
_____
_____
_____
_____
_____

There are lots of options. For instance, Alba might decide to talk to:

- a member of the Board about the lack of support for the new strategy
- the CFO about how she feels betrayed
- the CFO about his silence in earlier meetings
- the daughter about her access to the Board

How would you decide?

Deciding what you really want to talk about is the first step in having a HardTalk: you need some way of thinking about the whole scenario so that you can identify and prioritise all the issues. You don't want to waste your time having a HardTalk about the wrong subject(s).

Below, we walk through a three-step model designed to help you do just that.

THREE STEPS TO PRIORITISING

- *What Pains/Aches/Emergencies could you discuss?*
- *What results would make you happy?*
- *What do you complain about?*

Step 1: What Pains/Aches/Emergencies could you discuss?

DEFINITIONS

- **Pain:** *something that happens once*
- **Ache:** *something that happens repeatedly*
- **Emergency:** *something that's impacting your relationship*

Our first question helps you categorise the issues you are facing into one of three types: Pain | Ache | Emergency.

CHAPTER 1 | 10
LEARN TO RESPOND, NOT REACT

A Pain is something that happens once. It's fairly easy to deal with and most of us can have that conversation - maybe not well, but we can usually pick up the courage to say something if the result is important enough to us.

An Ache is different. This is when something happens again and again - there's a pain that just won't go away. In other words, you've spoken about a pain and it didn't get fixed. It's now turned into an ache.

Finally, there's an Emergency - this is the term we use when the issue is something that's impacting your relationship e.g. your ability to trust that person or rely on them.

Looking at the scenario and identifying the Pains, Aches and Emergencies helps us separate the different issues, and prioritise what to address.

The first step is in deciding whether you have a Pain, an Ache, or an Emergency on your hands - perhaps you might have more than one, or even more than one of each!

JUMANA

Jumana was frustrated. Adam had turned up dressed in jeans that morning. He'd apologised, explaining that the water in his apartment had been turned off and he'd just put a load of washing into the machine. Jumana wasn't sure what to think. There were often water shortages recently where Adam lived, but she knew that he spent a lot of his salary on clothes and didn't enjoy wearing the uniform the company provided. He'd never worn jeans to work before, but Jumana did remember telling him that his belt was too "flashy" and his shoes weren't appropriate as they were the wrong colour. He'd had an excuse on both those occasions too and she wasn't sure whether or not to believe him.

What are the Pains? Aches? Emergencies?

Pain *Adam is wearing incorrect uniform*

Ache *He has worn inappropriate clothes in the past*

Emergency *Jumana probably feels she can't trust him to tell the truth.*

Exercise:
Identify your Pains, Aches and Emergencies

Think about your own HardTalk scenario - the one you identified earlier. What Pains and Aches are you faced with? Do you have an Emergency?

Write your answers here.

_____
_____
_____
_____
_____
_____
_____
_____
_____
_____
_____
_____
_____
_____

WORKHARD 38

Answering these questions (What Pains and Aches are you faced with? Do you have an Emergency?) helps us break up the different issues. Maybe it's immediately obvious which issue should be raised. But the tendency is to go to the *easiest* one - the Pain.

Unfortunately, this just postpones the inevitable in many cases, and in others doesn't actually solve the problem. Instead, we go round in circles.

So how do you decide what to talk about once you've separated the issues?

Step two will help.

Step 2: What would make you happy?

Our next step is to answer the question: What *results would make you happy?* Think about what you want to get out of the conversation. What long-term results do you want in this scenario? For yourself? For the other person? For the project, team or organisation? Don't think about what's possible - just what you want.

Exercise:
What would make you happy?

Write your answers here:

_____
_____
_____
_____
_____
_____
_____
_____
_____
_____

Step 3: What do you complain about?

Here you're not being asked what you want to talk about. Or what you're prepared to bring up. Just to write down what's really bugging you.

It's another way of helping you to think about whether you'll be happy with the results you'll get if the conversation is a win. What do you complain about in your head? In the nasty email you fantasise about? When talking to your loved ones?

Exercise:
What do you complain about?

Write down all the things you complain about connected to your HardTalk scenario and then put them in order, with #1 being the thing that most bothers you, or is of most importance.

_____
_____
_____
_____
_____
_____
_____
_____
_____
_____

> **Deciding to speak up (or not) should be a response, not a reaction**

HardTalk is hard. We've acknowledged that, but we've also seen it's often worth it, and that nothing changes without it.

The question is: is it worth it in your case?

Nobody can answer this for you (see the *Rules of Adulting*) but what we can do is provide you with some *BrainTrains*, or exercises you can use to combat the *BrainDrains* that make it hard to speak up, or speak up effectively.

The idea is to get the rational part of our brain working - the executive part that can make good decisions, based on rational thought, and see the decision executed. And that's not easy because some things are *baked in*.

Human beings are not particularly cheery as a species. We tend to worry a lot. And not always about the right thing.

One way this comes out is when it comes to loss aversion. Loss aversion is how economists and decision theorists refer to our tendency to prefer avoiding losses than to acquiring the equivalent in gains. In other words, we don't feel loss and gain in the same way. That is what the research[11] shows us and if we consider it we realise it's true. We tend to feel loss more. We feel much more annoyance when we lose ten dollars than happiness when we gain it.

Put another way, the negative feelings coming from the loss are much stronger than the positive ones coming from the gain.

And we fear loss. We see this in marketing - people don't always buy because they want something - it's fear. The fear of missing out, it's even got its own acronym - FOMO[12].

> *FOMO: A pervasive apprehension that others might be having rewarding experiences from which one is absent*

We see this loss aversion play out as we decide whether or not to engage in HardTalk. Because we hate losing more than we enjoy winning, we may sit with the status quo rather than challenging it. We stay speechless, because we're more afraid of what we might lose, than we are excited about what we might gain.

KAREN

Karen, a relationship manager, worked in an international investment bank. She was excellent at her job. She knew her clients well and did her best for them using not only the bank's considerable resources but her own understanding of psychology to make sure she approached clients in the right way.

She understood how to help people make good financial decisions, and her success lead her to promotion until she managed a team of ten people across three geographical clusters. Her success now lay in making sure this group of people met their targets.

Instead of worrying about this, however, Karen focused on protecting her access to clients and senior management, ensuring she was seen as the font of all knowledge. Unsurprisingly her colleagues stopped trusting her and, ultimately, each other, and Karen's tenure was short-lived.

We're not good at working out what to be afraid of. Karen should have been afraid of not making the leap well into managing others, or of her client-facing skills not transferring. Instead, she worried about protecting access. This was her downfall. And it might be yours.

THE AVAILABILITY BIAS

When I ask groups of people to name something dangerous, the first or second answer is usually…SHARK!

(If this isn't what you came up with please do get in touch via www.hardtalk.info and tell us what you did think of!)

Here's the truth: In the United States, sharks kill on average one person every couple of years. The average number of people killed by texting, on the other hand, is 8 per day![13] But if you're asked to name something dangerous you will say shark (or something similar).

This is because of the availability bias: the tendency to make a decision based on the information that's most readily accessible in the brain, instead of taking into account the likelihood of this happening.

The easier it is to remember or imagine the consequences of something, the greater we perceive these consequences to be.

We find it much easier to recall instances of someone being killed by a shark - the images are more vivid – and, through books and movies, we have imagined being attacked by a shark. So we are more likely to think 'shark'.

This is fine, except it stops us making good decisions. The frequency with which events come to mind are usually not accurate reflections of the probabilities of such events in real life.

Texting is more dangerous than sharks.

The fact you're unlikely to think of it as more dangerous than sharks doesn't mean that it's not true.

This tendency can lead us to catastrophise - to think about the worst that could happen, and overestimate the likelihood of it happening.
The obvious impact of this *BrainDrain* on HardTalk is that we allow it to stop us having HardTalk - to *go speechless*.

We do this because we worry more about what we might lose than what there is to gain. We tend to worry about the worst case scenario (i.e. losing our job, self-respect or relationship).

Exercise:
Get more data and frame it

Use the exercises below to avoid falling into the traps our brains set for us:

One of the first things you can do to avoid reacting rather than responding is to stop and get more data.

Ask yourself:

If you have this HardTalk:

- What could go wrong?
- What's the worst case scenario?
- What's the likelihood of that scenario becoming reality?
- What could go right?
- What's the best case scenario?
- What's the likelihood of that scenario becoming reality?

_____
_____
_____
_____
_____
_____
_____

> *This tendency can lead us to catastrophise - to think about the worst that could happen, and overestimate the likelihood of it happening*

IS IT REALLY THAT LIKELY?

There are lots of ways of framing information.

The way you frame it will have an impact on the way that you think, feel and decide on resolutions.

For example, if I frame the gym as a way of getting you into shape so you can live long enough to see your children marry, that's different from framing it so it's about looking good for brunch or the beach.

You need to be able to frame the data in different ways, so you see the various angles and can make the most informed decision possible. This enables you to respond, rather than react.

You need to be aware of the way you're framing, and of the way others are framing for you.

We're all framing all the time. We tell our kids eating their vegetables will make them grow up big and strong. You could frame that differently and will do, depending on your filters. For example, in some places the frame might be *eat your vegetables* because we don't kill animals.

Can you think of any way you could re-frame your answers to the last exercise:

_____
_____
_____
_____
_____
_____
_____
_____
_____

RE-FRAME BY PERSPECTIVE

What would other people say the likelihood of a worst or best case scenario is? Choose five people who know you and your HardTalk partner, and ask them what they think the likelihood is, or imagine what their answers might be:

_____
_____
_____
_____
_____
_____

RE-FRAME BY ANCHORING

We tend to anchor to the first number we hear and, when we have lots of choices that's even truer (see the HardTalk blog for details of research), so anchor yourself away from this natural human tendency.[14]

Think about the most positive person you know. What would they say about your HardTalk partner? About the likelihood of a good outcome?

_____
_____
_____
_____
_____
_____
_____
_____
_____
_____

RE-FRAME BY TIME

Now write down the chances of the worst-case scenario happening:

_____
_____

Now imagine you have the conversation 10 times, what's the likelihood of it happening?

_____
_____

Now 100:

_____
_____

Now 1000:

_____
_____

If you're like most people, you'll find that the percentage likelihood has dropped. In other words, because you've imagined having many more opportunities to try you can imagine some of these being successful.

You get a more realistic view of success and might see your risk reduced to a level you feel more comfortable with. You might not. And, as we saw, not having HardTalk is absolutely an option. We just want to make sure that you're doing the deciding - that you're responding, and not just reacting.

RE-FRAME YOUR PURPOSE

Try to view the HardTalk in a light that makes you feel it worthwhile speaking up.

Remember it's a kindness to tell people bad news if hiding it doesn't stop them being affected by it, and it is possible to learn the skills to handle these conversations well.

REMAINING QUIET

There are consequences to remaining quiet, and they can be devastating.

I recently asked a senior leader to tell me the greatest professional regret he had. He told me that it was not giving a sales guy immediate, useful feedback about how he came across to the high net worth individuals they were targeting.

'Honestly, I really liked the guy, and didn't want to be the one to tell him that I couldn't see him ever being successful at this,' he told me. As a result, his sales employee missed out on valuable feedback and potentially wasted years doing something he was never going to be great at.

Eventually, he was fired. Even more tragically, the next time my contact saw the guy, he was homeless and begging on a street corner.

WHATEVER YOUR RESPONSE, THERE WILL BE CONSEQUENCES

It's up to you to do the math(s) and make the decision about whether to have the conversation or not. Nobody else can tell you if the risk/reward ratio makes sense. It's about the results that you want to get; the risk you're willing to take, and the stuff you're prepared to put up with.

It doesn't mean you get to be rude - that has an impact on performance too. For example, in a medical operating room staffed with highly-qualified, professional and experienced medical teams, studies have shown they underperform by about 50 per cent when confronted with a rude *expert* giving unsolicited feedback.[15]

It doesn't mean you'll always *win*. Not everyone will always be convinced. Some people are poor performers or ill-suited for the job; some people will never perform at the level you need.

But if you can build an environment where everyone is heard, you are likely to have better relationships, deal more effectively with underperformance, and make better decisions in a more motivated, healthy work environment.

CHAPTER 1 | 10
LEARN TO RESPOND, NOT REACT

ONLY TWO OPTIONS
- You can make any decision you like but you must live with the consequences
- Every action is a decison

FIVE OUTCOMES
- Do nothing and be miserable
- Do nothing and make that your decision, and focus on something else
- Do something and run a risk and see things get better
- Do something and run a risk and see things stay the same
- Do something and run a risk and see things get worse

Not speaking up means deciding to be speechless. It's your decision but staying speechless has risks too:

BEING SPEECHLESS
- Silence is consent
- Silence may harm others
- Silence will stop your filters being acknowledged
- Silence hides your worth
- Silence may lose you friends and followers

Going Speechless can make your life harder in a number of ways. Primarily, nothing changes unless somebody speaks up. Then there's the rest:

Silence is deemed approval.
You may think going Speechless keeps you from being involved in any conflict, but that's not the case. By not speaking up you're taking a position. If the problem persists and you did nothing, people may consider it as enabling, and think the issue is as much your fault as the person who actually caused the problem.

Most of us are speechless because we don't want to do any harm by offending or criticising someone.
But when you see a person or the team doing something dangerous it's selfish not to speak up - you may be harming the very people you hope to help. Author and team management expert Patrick Lencioni[16] calls it telling people *the kind truth* because...

No one else may know.
You can't assume the obvious is obvious. No one else has your unique perspective - nobody else sees things through your filters. In fact they see the world through their own particular filters and may be unaware of the impact they're having.

Show your worth.
Why are you in the conversation in the first place? You're involved for a reason. If you truly don't have a stake, then find a better use of your time. But if you are there for a reason, you need to show your commitment to the process and the people involved by being active and vocal. Because you never know.

You may not be alone in your thinking.
It's entirely possible your insightful observations and conclusions have surfaced in the minds of others. Others may share

WORKHARD 44

your thoughts and opinions but may be also unwilling to speak up. By speaking your mind you encourage them to voice their opinions as well.

If everyone holds back, the bus may silently head over a cliff.

DON'T GO SPEECHLESS IF IT'S GOING TO ERUPT

If you do decide to stay speechless that's more than fine - you're an adult. Just don't go speechless as the default, and remember you must live with the consequences. If you don't speak up you must let it go.

In other words, you can decide that the potential downside or *doom* is just too much and "let it go"; but you have to really let it go - not gossip, whinge, avoid or make hints because those activities lead to appalling results for you and for others.

You can't hold on, give the issue time in your head, complain or let your emotions about it colour other things.

That's hard! Can you really do that?

If you can't - if your boss' micromanaging really does eat away at you, or your spouse's unwillingness to communicate drives you truly crazy and you can't *let it go*; then you need to have the HardTalk. If you really can't, you need to consider your position and think about your next move.

If you've worked through the exercises and still decided not to speak (for good reasons) then we hope you will be able to "let it go". But if you've just pushed down something you really feel should be raised, then beware!

Don't stay speechless and risk an eruption. Sometimes we *make the decision* not to speak up, and don't manage to let it go.

Eventually, the pressure is too great, and we explode. In that moment, almost inevitably, we handle the conversation or HardTalk in the worst way possible, confirming our sense that we were right to be afraid in the first place. Don't do this.

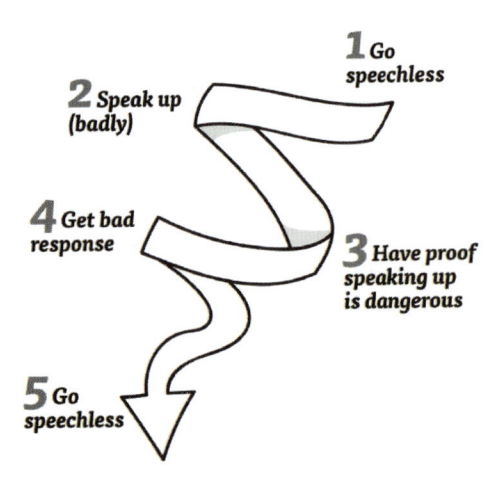

1 Go speechless
2 Speak up (badly)
3 Have proof speaking up is dangerous
4 Get bad response
5 Go speechless

Get control of your emotions and build your self-awareness instead.

CHAPTER SUMMARY

- "We often don't speak up because we want to be nice, are risk adverse and don't like feeling uncomfortable"

- "But if we want great results we need to have difficult conversations"

- "As adults you can make your own decisions but you must live with the consequences. Silence has consequences too"

- "HardTalk is hard because of three elements: Difference, Topic and Purpose"

- "Our differences mean our filters are different, which makes how we interpret Truths very different"

- "Deciding what you want to address ie the Topic of the HardTalk is harder than you think"

- "You need to identify if you have an Ache, Pain or an Emergency – or maybe more than one!"

- "Speaking up or not speaking up both have consequences – make sure you are framing correctly to evaluate the potential outcome of both decisions/actions."

CONTROL YOUR EMOTIONS

CHAPTER 2

Emotions are inevitable. The more you pretend otherwise, the more you're at their mercy. We must learn how to control our emotions, so we can manage our behaviour in HardTalk scenarios.

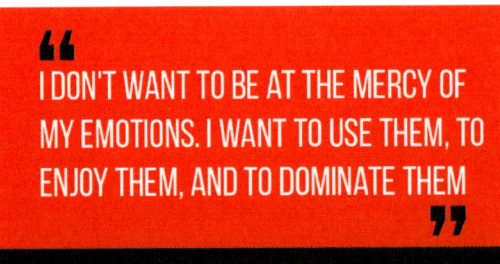

> **I DON'T WANT TO BE AT THE MERCY OF MY EMOTIONS. I WANT TO USE THEM, TO ENJOY THEM, AND TO DOMINATE THEM**
>
> Oscar Wilde, Writer

We all have emotions. That's pretty much the definition of being human. They are, as we'll see, the fuel for behaviour

This chapter does not try to help you avoid or "deal with" your emotions. Instead, it's about being aware of the emotions you're experiencing and *making a decision* about how to use them. It's about emotional intelligence or, to use a more old-fashioned phrase, self-possession.

Seventeenth-century philosopher Benedict de Spinoza observed that *"an emotion, which is a passion, ceases to be a passion as soon as we form a clear and distinct idea thereof. [The emotion] becomes more under our control, and the mind is less passive in respect to it."*[17]

In other words, being aware of our emotions can help us manage them. There is a complex relationship between thoughts, moods, brain chemistry, endocrine function, and the functioning of other physiological systems in our bodies. While an in-depth discussion of this relationship is beyond the scope of this book, it's enough to say our thoughts can trigger physiological changes.

Self-possession: having or showing control of your feelings or actions, especially in a difficult situation

Let's take one emotion that often crops up in HardTalk scenarios - anger

Darin Dougherty, an HMS associate professor of psychiatry at Massachusetts General Hospital, put healthy patients into a PET scan and asked them to remember incidents in their lives that had made them angry.[18]

When they did this the *amygdala* (the *"lizard"* or *"monkey"* brain) could be seen to fire up but, at the same time, a part of the orbital frontal cortex (the *"executive"* brain) also engaged. This activation allowed the subjects to control their anger. However, people with depression saw only the amygdala get involved and, as a result, they continued to feel angry and to act on it. These people were not in control of their feelings - they were not self-possessed.

This is important because your emotions don't just impact how you behave - that behaviour will, in turn, influence others. For example, Martin Teicher, Associate Professor of Psychiatry at Harvard Medical School, found that verbal abuse from parents and peers causes changes in developing brains with deleterious effects on a par with witnessing domestic violence and other seemingly more violent forms of maltreatment.[19]

He says *"anger is a big problem. It's a problem when we express it too much and when we express it too little."*

So how can we control our emotions?

Many years ago, I went home to visit my family over the Christmas holiday. A dislike of shopping meant I arrived, as the Irish say, "hands hanging". I borrowed my father's new car, despite my driving capabilities being known to him (including the fact I failed my test four times before finally passing) and successfully bought the necessary presents.

Driving down a road near my parent's home I noticed a huge, wrought-iron gate - a kind of "Downton Abbey" deal. The gates were open, and a very large, very black, very expensive looking car suddenly appeared. It was driving in the middle of the road and it was driving fast. I assumed the driver would notice me at any moment. But he continued at the same pace and in the same position - in the centre of the road. He was moving very fast. Suddenly I realised that it wasn't going to slow down or pull over. I swerved wildly and slammed on the brakes, ending up on the side of the road. I was shaken and, more than anything else, furious.

Despite my own limitations as a driver, I'm safe. I wouldn't drive if I weren't. I was in a horrible accident as a child and car safety is something I take seriously. I don't like bad drivers. And I really don't like drivers who drive as if they own the road. Particularly if they have big cars.

I calmed myself down as best as I could and drove the short distance home. Of course, my mother knew something was wrong as soon as she saw me (mothers always know!) and listened as I started to tell her what had happened.

"You'll never believe it," I said. "I was a few minutes away when suddenly this big car came out of nowhere and drove straight at me."

"Was it near the big gates?" my mother asked.

I was nonplussed. Why would she care where it happened? Where was the outrage? Ah, I got it.

"What? This has happened before? Is this guy known to do this? That's crazy. I'm calling the police!" I jumped up to get the phone.

"What are you talking about? What guy?" My mother stopped me. "Those gates are the entrance to a critical care and end-of-life unit, so we know to drive very carefully around there - many of the people coming out will be having one of the worst days of their lives, and may not be paying attention."

My mood changed abruptly. I was no longer full of righteous anger. Instead, I was sad and resolved to be more careful when driving in that neighbourhood (unlikely to happen anytime soon if my father heard about my near miss!). What had happened to make me change my mind about what the right thing to do - the right action - was? Easy. I had new information that moved me back down the "Ladder to Action" and allowed me to see that the world wasn't necessarily as I saw it through my filters.

Our actions don't come from nowhere. If you want to be in control of your actions, then you need to be in control of your emotions - and that means understanding where they come from.

Controlling our emotions is key to having successful HardTalk - we need to be in control, so we can act in ways that help us rather than stop us from getting what we want.

Here's one of the big ideas in HardTalk - there's a *"Ladder to Action"* that we all climb. And we climb it fast. We climb it so fast we're not even aware we're climbing it. As we climb or rather fly, up this ladder, we pass through a number of phases.

5 ACTION
4 EMOTION
3 POTENTIAL
2 FILTER
1 TRUTH

As humans when we see and hear something - we notice a Truth.

> ### A Truth is what we see and hear

We see and hear a Truth (or Truths) and then tell ourselves a story based on those Truths. That *story* will be influenced by many things - by our *filters*, by our experience.

In the story about the dangerous driver, my filters initially lead me to feel righteous fury and indignation, and so want to call the police. When I was (luckily) given more information, my filters changed, and the *Potential* I immediately came up with changed.

So, we notice a Truth, we hear or see something, and it goes through our filters and we come up with a story. And of course, it's not the only story we could tell based on those Truths. It's only one *Potential*.

For example, we might notice that the person delivering the HardTalk training is sitting on the table as he talks to the room of participants.

If a typical middle-aged Japanese person saw a trainer sitting on the desk they would likely feel ashamed, embarrassed, perhaps a little annoyed. It's not culturally acceptable in Japan to sit on a desk.

Because of different filters, a typical young American would be likely to see the same Truth and come up with a different *Potential* – perhaps simply that the trainer was relaxed or even tired.

> ### A Potential is a judgement we make about the truth, based on our filters

CHAPTER 2 | 10
CONTROL YOUR EMOTIONS

There are always many Potentials. We know this because if we had different filters we would probably come up with different potentials.

The Potential we "choose" is the one *in charge* though. It leads to an emotion and then that emotion leads to an action. So if we want to manage action - our own or someone else's - we need to manage the emotions. That means acknowledging there are lots of different potentials.

Exercise:
Can you spot the Truths?

Danica was worried about her colleague Anya. Anya was less motivated than she used to be, turning up late to many meetings in the last week, and actually failing to attend the "optional" weekly lunch. Danica had heard that she'd had a fight with another colleague about something trivial, and was now being discussed as unstable by HR.

What Truths can you spot?

_____
_____
_____
_____
_____
_____
_____
_____
_____
_____
_____
_____
_____

There are only three Truths in the story above, i.e:

- Anya turned up late to a number of meetings
- Anya didn't attend the weekly lunch
- Danica has heard some rumours

A Potential is the story we tell ourselves about the Truth given, once it's gone through all our filters. So, for example, given the "Truth" "she turned up late" you could come up with any number of "potentials". For example, your filters might lead you to feel that she:

- is lazy
- is disorganised
- had an accident
- was dealing with a sick kid
- is unmotivated
- doesn't know how to get to work on time

Exercise:
What Potentials can you come up with?

For each of the following Truths please give one positive and one negative Potential.

1. *Your co-worker is wearing the same clothes as yesterday*

2. *Your boss has asked you three times today how things are going on a report not due until next week*

3. *You did not receive your usual courtesy invitation to the quarterly executive team offsite*

_____
_____
_____
_____
_____
_____
_____
_____
_____
_____

WORKHARD   50

But beware - somehow there is a tendency to go negative first - it's the doom-monger in us!

You'll notice the assumption that people will always make the worst assumption is a trope in many movies and novels.

Some scientists would say it's because in the past we evolved to avoid danger rather than investigate it.[20] Investigating that rustle in the bush was just too risky, so we learned to avoid it and to assume the worst possible outcome.

But that reflex doesn't help us. We need to respond and not react. We need to control our emotions. We're still allowed to have emotions - we just need to recognise where they come from. We need to slow down our ascent of the *"Ladder of Action"* and allow for the possibility that the emotion we're feeling, although real, is not the only possible reaction. Gaining that insight gives us some control and a chance to regain self-possession.

We move very quickly from the Truth to the Potential that seems most likely to us (based on our filters) and that makes us feel an emotion. Then we behave as that emotion tells us to! We don't behave in a way that gets us the long-term results we want.

We don't behave as though our executive brains are in charge, because they're not. To manage that, we need to be able to spot the difference between Truths and Potentials. It's harder than you think, and even harder in real life, when emotions are running strong.

Exercise:
Stick to the Truths and watch out for the Potentials

In each of the following scenarios, you are presented with at least one Truth and only one Potential. Can you separate the two?

1. You enter the communal bathroom at the office, see a colleague exiting a stall and only stopping to check their hair in the mirror. You feel disgusted at their lack of hygiene.

2. Your boss has given you a piece of work that you could do with your eyes closed. Despite this, the brief she gave you was very detailed. She has checked in 5 times already, despite the deadline being a week away, making you feel like she doesn't trust you.

3. Your direct report checked her phone half a dozen times during your weekly "huddle" this morning and has not completed some paperwork you have made clear is important. You're starting to feel she doesn't respect you.

Can you come up with another positive Potential for each of these?

_____
_____
_____
_____
_____
_____
_____
_____
_____
_____
_____
_____

Being aware of our tendency to see Potentials as reality is a first step in controlling our emotions. As you'll see later, we're not saying we're always wrong in our Potential nor that our filters aren't useful - they're the sum of our experience and more. Of course they are sometimes useful - but we need to be aware that they are there, so we are not fooled into thinking our Potential is a Truth.

STICK TO THE TRUTHS AND WATCH OUT FOR THE POTENTIALS

It is important to stick to the Truths because they are conclusive. They are what you saw and heard. They are non-negotiable. If you were filming, you would be able to see them. They are the baseline. If they are not accepted, then there's no point in going any further.

It wasn't really until the 12th century that the idea of a fact caught on in England because of the development of trial by jury.[21] *Only from the law did it then spread out over the following six centuries to science, history, journalism and now, we are hoping, to conversation!*

Why are Potentials dangerous?

They create emotions, quickly

They leave no place to learn

So we've seen how to stick to the Truths. Now we must watch out for Potentials. Why?

There are three main reasons to watch out for Potentials.

Firstly, they create emotions, quickly. If we only see one Potential (and probably a negative one) then we see it as a Truth. And that means there's no way to "short circuit" the *"ladder to action"* or process of **Truths - Filters - Potentials - Emotion – Action**, and so allow us to manage our *Action*.

This is fundamental because the only point of reading this book and working on HardTalk skills is to change your action - because that's the only way you change your results.

Secondly, Potentials are dangerous because they bring us very quickly to thinking we know what the problem is, and so trying to fix it. This is usually a colossal waste of time, as we find out we were trying to fix the wrong problem or a problem that the other person doesn't see as a problem.

Finally, Potentials that aren't recognised as such are dangerous because they allow us to believe we are "right", which is unlikely to be helpful. It doesn't leave you any room to learn if you think you already know. It destroys the curiosity you need to have a successful HardTalk.

We need to watch out for the Potentials. Certainty is the enemy when entering a HardTalk: if you already know everything then why are you bothering to have the conversation?

Not noticing our Potentials is just one of many possibilities that stops us being curious, and from being in control. Think about it: if you can come up with six reasons why Ramy didn't invite you to the meeting last week, aren't you likely to start the conversation more curious than anything else?

If we can be more curious - about the reasons behind the other's behaviour (and our own), and humbler about our certainty, as we acknowledge not everyone in the world sees things in the same way we do, this will naturally put us in the constructive frame of mind that is most likely to help in a difficult conversation.

Asking questions is a good thing to do. Even if no new information is uncovered, it "kickstarts" the brain and gets the "executive" brain working again. And puts "you" back in control.

What positive and negative **"Potentials"** can you come up with for these Truths? Try to give at least two of each for each Truth.

_____
_____
_____
_____
_____
_____
_____
_____
_____
_____
_____
_____

This isn't a magic bullet, but it's a powerful tool, so let's look at the Truths and watch out for the Potentials in your HardTalk Scenario.

Exercise:
Your HardTalk scenario - identify the Truths and Potentials

What **"Truths"** can you identify in your HardTalk scenario? What did you see and hear that is relevant to what you want to discuss?

_____
_____
_____
_____
_____
_____
_____
_____

SELF-AWARENESS IS KEY TO SELF-POSSESSION

Brains are weird. Put your right foot out in front of you and turn it in a clockwise direction. Repeat a number of times. As you continue to do that use the index finger of your right hand to write the number six in the air. Notice what happens to your foot. Nobody really seems sure why this is so, but it's likely a by-product of something useful.

Faced with a HardTalk scenario we feel a lot of emotions. We might feel angry, guilty, worried, nervous - nobody wants to, or could, stop you having these emotions. They are natural and normal and we need to feel things so we can respond appropriately.

But we also need to recognise they are there and, that they can have control over us.

When emotions are in control, they are focused on what feels good right now. Instead,

CHAPTER 2
CONTROL YOUR EMOTIONS

you (your executive brain) needs to be in control - you want to be focused on your long-term purpose - the results you care about. You need to control those emotions, and that's not easy.

Have you ever overreacted? for example, have you ever felt...

so happy that you gave away something you shouldn't have?

so frustrated you undid weeks of hard work building a relationship by snapping?

so annoyed that you overreacted and gave a secret away in a meeting?

It's easy to lose control. We all do it. How many people do you think wake up *meaning* to shout at their kids, or lose their temper with their spouse over something small, or insult their colleague by taking a call when they're speaking, or shut down a direct report by rolling their eyes because they're irritated? Very few, right? Yet it happens. All the time.

We lose "it" - we lose our self-possession. We are, quite literally, no longer in possession of our "self". No longer am "I" in control – instead, my emotions take over and my executive brain stops working so well. It becomes all about what feels good right now.

You've felt this, haven't you? If not, then you are excused from reading the rest of this chapter. In fact, if your emotions never ever get the best of you, please get in touch and tell us your secret!

Emotions are inevitable, and the more you pretend otherwise the more you're at their mercy. When you think about it, it makes sense that when you are feeling a certain emotion, you behave differently.

Remember there are lots of emotions. You might feel one or more of any of them including, but certainly not limited to...

Amazed Angry Annoyed Anxious Ashamed Bitter Bored Comfortable Confused Content Depressed Determined Disdainful Disgusted Eager Embarrassed Energetic Envious Excited Foolish Frustrated Furious Grieving Happy Hopeful Hurt Inadequate Insecure Inspired Irritated Jealous Joyful Lonely Lost Loving Miserable Motivated Nervous Overwhelmed Peaceful Proud Relieved Resentful Sad Satisfied Scared Self-conscious Shocked Silly Stupid Suspicious Tense Terrified Trapped Uncomfortable Worried Worthless

We often believe our emotions are justified, correct, or obvious. Then, because of our filters, we find out there are perfectly lovely people who, faced with the same situation we are in, would not feel the same emotion and would behave differently.

> *"We don't see things as they are, we see them as we are"*
> — Anais Nin, Writer

There are people who seem to be able to manage their behaviour despite feeling emotion. They can, in the midst of a HardTalk scenario, remember to stick to the Truths and watch out for the Potentials. They can focus on what they want long-term. How do they do that?

Well, they certainly don't tell themselves to calm down! Have you tried telling someone to calm down? What happens next is rarely a moment of calm. Instead, people like FBI negotiators are trained to be able to recognise and name that emotion, ask themselves why they find themselves feeling that way, and whether it's appropriate.

Doing all of that moves us, as we'll see in the next Chapter, from System 1 to System 2

WORKHARD 54

thinking, (puts our brain back into gear), and allows us to "take the heat out", so we can deal with the HardTalk effectively, and decide how to portray that emotion so that the other person can understand it.

To control our "selves", to be in possession, means we must first notice we are not in charge. This means we need to be very self-aware.

If I showed you a film of two people in a HardTalk scenario you'd probably have lots of sensible things to say about how well they did, and good advice to give.

Yet, like me, you probably get it wrong more often than you'd like. Knowing how to behave isn't the key. Being self-aware enough to move from unconscious incompetence to conscious incompetence on the "Ladder of Learning" *is* key:

It means noticing the results you are getting, and deciding whether they match what you want, and then being capable of making different choices. We call this the *Process of Progress*.

Process of Progress

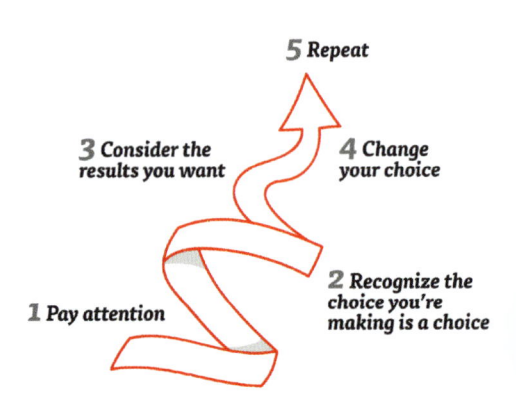

5 *Repeat*

3 *Consider the results you want*

4 *Change your choice*

1 *Pay attention*

2 *Recognize the choice you're making is a choice*

Ladder of Learning

Unconscious Competence — You do things without thinking about them

practice

Conscious Competence — You know what you're doing

intervention

Conscious Incompetence — You are aware of your lack of knowledge

feedback

Unconscious Incompetence — You don't know that you don't know

MAKING IT STICK

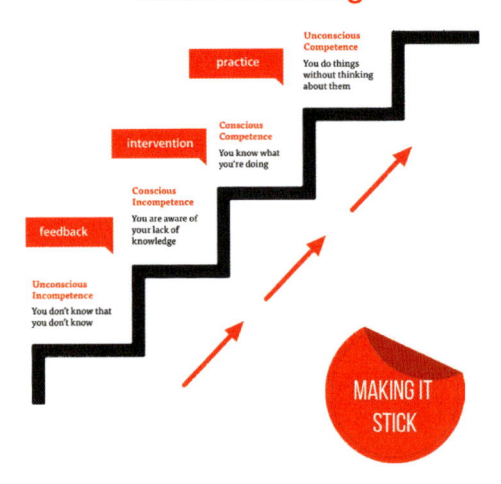

Self-awareness requires *practice with self-monitoring*, and *getting feedback*.

It means being open to criticism, and not being defensive.

NAMING EMOTIONS IS A WAY OF CONTROLLING THEM

When people in an MRI machine were shown photos of faces expressing strong emotions their amygdala lit up.[22] As we mentioned earlier, this is the part of the brain involved in generating emotions, so that makes sense. But when tasked to name the emotion, activity in their amygdala dropped, and there was more activity in a region of the right frontal lobe known as the right ventrolateral pre-frontal cortex (rvPFC) - the region involved in vigilance and discrimination.

It seems that assessing and naming an emotion seems to transform the emotion into an object of scrutiny, thereby disrupting its raw intensity.

Based on this research, we suggest *naming your emotion*.

CHAPTER 2 | 10
CONTROL YOUR EMOTIONS

THE BOOK OF HUMAN EMOTIONS

Tiffany Watt Smith, a researcher at the Centre for the History of the Emotions at Queen Mary University of London, has written about difficult-to-define emotions from many cultures in her book ***The Book of Human Emotions***[23]

"When we're talking about what an emotion is, it's easy for us to fall into the trap of thinking that emotions are just physiological responses to external stimuli, and that we all pretty much have exactly the same sort of responses, and these are primarily happening in our body," Watt Smith said. *"But actually, they're not. Emotions are much more flexible and malleable things, and they are happening in conversation with the way we think about what they are, and how we name them, and how we make sense of them."*

Exercise:
Name the emotions

What emotions do you feel going into your HardTalk scenario? Labelling, or naming, the emotion you're feeling has an impact on your ability to control the effect the emotion has on your behaviour. Thinking of your HardTalk scenario, choose five emotions you feel and arrange them in order of strength. Get granular - the more specific you can be the better! You can use the list on *page 84* to help you or choose your own...

_____
_____
_____
_____
_____
_____

Playing video games can help you control emotions

Self-awareness is hard. When the emotions are kicking in and you're about to start reacting rather than responding, you need to be aware and have strategies to help you back to the right path.

One way you can practice, if you can get your hands on it, is by playing a game called *Rage Control* (Regulate and Gain Emotional Control), a video game developed by psychiatrists at Harvard University.[24]

Originally designed for young people, it tracks your heart rate as enemy spaceships attack - and disables your shooter when it perceives you getting angry or overexcited. The idea is that, over time, you learn what your body feels like when you're losing control, and how to calm yourself to stay within your resting heart rate.

This process strengthens the connection between the brain's executive control *(pre-frontal cortex)* and emotional area *(amygdala)*, much in the way meditation does.

The advantage of this over meditation or bio-feedback training is that it doesn't ask you to leave the situation. It's more practical because it's about staying calm during something frustrating, and so is much more realistic.

IDENTIFYING THE LIFEMORTS CAN HELP YOU GET OVER RAGE

In HardTalk situations where strong emotions are in play, we can often overreact. The kind of impulsive, feels-good-right-now behaviour we exhibit tends not to be the most helpful in achieving our long-term goals, and others may often struggle to understand what happened.

R. Douglas Fields, a senior investigator at the

WORKHARD 56

National Institute of Health has worked out why we overreact, and for a very good reason - he wanted to understand why road rage happens.[25]

Fields argues that there are nine major triggers that invoke a rage response, which he has assembled into the acronym LIFEMORTS: Life and limb, as in your physical safety; Insult, meaning a verbal threat. The next six are self-explanatory: Family, Environment, Mate, Order in society, Resources, Tribe - you already know each of these are things you'd fight for if you felt they were in danger.

The last word is Stopped. This is the idea that any animal (humans included) will ready itself to fight if it feels restrained or trapped (this explains road rage!). So for each of these nine triggers, the rage kicks in to prepare you for a potential fight, because you feel like something essential has been threatened.

LIFEMORTS

LIFEMORTS are nine triggers identified by neuroscience as causing us to lose our temper and self-control: Life and Limb, Insult, Family, Environment, Mate, Order In Society, Resources, Tribe, Stopped.

"It's not conscious, and it happens rapidly. So this is part of the brain's threat-detection response mechanism. When we're confronted with a common threat, we have the neural circuitry to respond quickly and aggressively to that threat. That neural circuitry is all subcortical; it's not conscious. If you dodge a basketball, it comes flying into your peripheral vision, and you react. This is actually a really complex motor reaction, where you will duck, raise your hand, close your eyes - all of that happens before you're aware of it.

So what's happening here is that an enormous portion of the brain is devoted to threat detection - that system runs from the pre-frontal cortex to the amygdala to the hypothalamus, all the way across the brain. And this threat-detection mechanism is constantly taking in information from all of our senses, every one of them - and internal senses, too - constantly assessing the situation in our internal and external environment for threats. So this information streams into that subcortical part of the brain before it ever goes to our conscious brain.

And the minute something is received as dangerous, or threatening, it invokes this defensive physical reaction. That's the connection between snapping and threat detection, and that explains why we're bewildered after we react in this way. Because just in the same way that you will dodge a basketball before you even consciously know it's coming, or jump out of the way of a car that narrowly misses you in a parking lot - it's the same kind of feeling when you, you know, start using purple language because somebody cuts in front of you on the highway. It's that same feeling. Both of those situations have tripped defensive circuits in the brain."

R. Douglas Fields

Having identified the LIFEMORTS, Fields asked Secret Service agents and members of SEAL Team 6 how they control themselves when faced with threats like these. They said the most important thing is to notice when LIFEMORTS are at play. Understanding the mechanism helps to control it: it's not enough but it's the most important first step.

Telling yourself to calm down, trying to suppress that emotion, counting to three - these things don't work. What does work is (again it comes back to self-monitoring and self-awareness) noticing you're feeling angry, upset, revengeful, disappointed or whatever, and asking yourself *"Where in the LIFEMORTS do I feel threatened?"* and then, *"Is this a reasonable response?"*

This forces you to go to the Truths and to question your Potentials.

> Notice how you're feeling and behaving and ask *"Where in the LIFEMORTS do I feel threatened?"* and *"Is this a reasonable response?"*

Exercise:
Which LIFEMORTS might be at risk in your HardTalk scenario?

When I was forced to veer off the road in order to avoid what I thought was a maniac in a big, black car, it's pretty clear the LIFEMORTS at risk was L - Life and Limb.
What about your HardTalk scenario?

_____
_____
_____
_____
_____
_____
_____
_____
_____

PREPARING IN ADVANCE AVOIDS THE "HOT STATE" PERILS

When Ulysses faced the peril of the Sirens and their irresistible songs, he used what a behavioural economist came to call *"cold state"* to prepare for *"hot state"*[26]. In other words, he prepared in advance.

Ulysses instructed his crew to fill their ears with wax so they would not be tempted by the music and the emotions it created. He also asked the crew to tie him to the mast so that he could listen for himself but be restrained from submitting to the temptation to steer the ship closer when the music put him into a hot state.

This is why, when you're on a weight-loss diet, it's a good idea to have healthy snacks and no call out menus or delivery apps. We'll use the HardTalk model and particularly the Decision Tree *(see Chapter 1)* to do this as we prepare for HardTalk.

HAVE AN IF/THEN PLAN
LOOKING FROM A DIFFERENT PERSPECTIVE CAN ADD TO YOUR TRUTHS

The International Handbook of Anger by Gerben A. Van Kleef[27] concluded that anger leads to less successful outcomes in negotiation - a certain kind of "application" of HardTalk - and this was true whether you are angry at the other party, or the other party is angry at you.

Remembering what you want in the long-term (as we'll see in *Chapter 5 Remember Your Purpose*) helps, and so does having an *"if/then"* plan e.g. *"if she refuses to speak to me, then I'll ask when she is next free,"* and *"if she can't say, then I'll ask when it's best to ask next."*

Exercise:
What if/then might you use in your HardTalk scenario?

_____
_____

Exercise:
In your HardTalk scenario how does looking at it from the perspective of a fly on the wall help? Can you see any more Truths?

Controlling your emotions so you remain self-possessed - in control of your actions - is key to successful HardTalk. It's not easy, but you now have gained six tools you can use to improve:

- Stick to the Truths and watch out for the Potentials
- Name your emotions to control them
- Identify the LIFEMORTS to get over rage
- Avoid the 'Hot State' perils by preparing in advance
- Have an If/Then plan
- Use the 'fly on the wall' perspective to spot Truths you might have missed

Adding some perspective adds to the Truths and Potentials

As any police officer will tell you, if you ask three people to explain what just happened you'll get three different answers. Because you'll get three different perspectives. The perspective we have - the Potentials we can see - change our emotions and this changes our action.

We want to see lots of Potentials so we can manage our emotions, and so our behaviours.

*One way to do this, when you notice you're feeling a lot of emotion, is to replay the event from a fly on the wall perspective so that you focus on the Truths and move away from Potentials. This ability to **"self-distance"** makes people calmer and less vindictive.*

In other words, more in control.

CHAPTER SUMMARY

- *"To have successful HardTalk we must have self-possession and be in control of our emotions"*
- *"We must be aware of climbing the Ladder to Action – Truth, Filter, Potential, Emotion, Action"*
- *"Truths are facts – what we see and hear. Potentials are how we interpret those facts based on our filters and how other people interpret them based on theirs"*
- *"Potentials can be dangerous as they create emotions that, if not managed, will cause us to act in negative ways"*
- *"Naming emotions is a way of controlling them"*
- *"Use the LIFEMORTS – Life and limb, Insult, Family, Environment, Mate, Order in society, Resources, Tribe, Stopped to identify your feelings and whether your response is correct and going to get you the results you want"*
- *"Use the six tools to improve your self-possession, which you will need throughout HardTalk"*

BEWARE THE PATTERN

CHAPTER 3

Patterns are dangerous. Not wallpaper ones of course, but the ones our lazy brains love to use to create shortcuts. Our brains are filled with these shortcuts and biases, that we aren't even aware of, and they cause us to make costly mistakes.

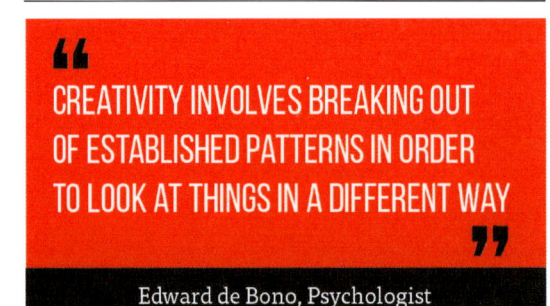

> **CREATIVITY INVOLVES BREAKING OUT OF ESTABLISHED PATTERNS IN ORDER TO LOOK AT THINGS IN A DIFFERENT WAY**
>
> Edward de Bono, Psychologist

WE ARE ALL TWO PEOPLE: ONE OF THEM REALLY LIKES PATTERNS

Have you ever automatically reacted when your name is called? Found yourself picking up a cigarette or cup of coffee without planning to? Suffered through irrationally disliking someone (just a little) because their name is the same as a person you once had a bad experience with? (hello Sheena!).

This is what we like to call the 'Homer Simpson brain' *(from The Simpsons cartoon)* or *'System 1'* thinking. This Homer brain tells us where to sit, when to shake hands, what to say when someone hands us a menu, and how to respond when someone asks: *"How are you?"*

It's unfair to call this system 'stupid', but we can certainly say it's no better than automatic pilot. However automatic it might be, it is very helpful, as we simply don't have the "bandwidth" to make the hundreds of thousands of decisions thrown at us every day.

System 1 thinking allows us to make quick decisions based on very little information. The fleeting impressions and the numerous shortcuts you've developed combine to allow quick decisions to be made without deliberation or conscious effort. Our "Homer" brain finds patterns and uses these to make decisions automatically.

CHAPTER 3 | 10
BEWARE THE PATTERN

Remember, these are not based on value judgements, just on experience – both good and bad.

System 1 type thought makes us freeze when we see a spider or a shadow move in the corner of our eye. It's automatic. It's what 'feels' right based on what we've experienced in the past. It's what we're used to. It's the reason why, if you're white and Western European, you're likely to eat curry happily in the evening but find the thought of it when you just wake up distasteful – it's just not what you're used to.

Homer is a useful brain to have around; just not in HardTalk when we need to be on our best, most reflective behaviour and not some kind of *Pavlovian dog* wannabe!

Ivan Pavlov and the Dogs[28]

In the early 1900s Russian physiologist, Ivan Pavlov ran a series of experiments with dogs. He discovered that a neutral stimulus, such as a bell, could result in a conditioned response from the dogs – i.e. they would start to salivate upon hearing the bell as they had learned to associate it with food.

System 1: The Doer

- ■ *Fast*
- ■ *Automatic*
- ■ *Effortless*
- ■ *Impulsive*
- ■ *Involuntary*
- ■ *Always "on"*

But the "Homer Brain" is not alone. Oh no, we're two people. We're Homer, but we're also "Spock" *(from the Star Trek TV show and films)*. We're System 1, the myopic 'Doer' and System 2, the far-sighted 'Planner'.

System 2: The Planner

- ■ *Slow*
- ■ *Deliberate*
- ■ *Effortful*
- ■ *Wiser*
- ■ *Voluntary parts of our brains*
- ■ *Processes suggestions offered by System 1*
- ■ *Makes final decisions and chooses where to allocate our attention*

Spock is the logical part of us, the far-sighted planner of System 2. The executive brain, System 2 stops and 'thinks': categorising, comparing, considering and then consciously deciding to take one path or another.

Our "Spock Brain" can imagine a future beyond the next 30 minutes and can make decisions based on what is most likely to make that future a reality.

While Homer would return from the store with whatever most appealed to him in the moment, or whatever he would normally buy; Spock would have a list and make decisions based on weighted criteria including nutritional value, seasonality, price and even any associated Air Miles or loyalty points.

WORKHARD

At any time, our brains are capable of being *either* Homer or Spock, with the "Spock Brain" clearly taking more effort. This means that unless we make a concerted effort, our brains will revert to System 1 automatically. We are animals – we are programmed to use as little effort as possible; which in turn means that we rely on experience and patterns.

PATTERN

A model or design used as a guide

Being Spock is tough on our neurological systems, meaning we do our best to avoid it. This also means that in HardTalk scenarios it's one of the first things to be decommissioned, as our bodies focus our energy on fighting or flying. It's not easy to fight against our tendency to rely on our "Homer brains" (System 1) but it is possible.

If we care about results, we need to learn how to do this.

Look at the picture. Before you read any more, look at it again quickly.

What do you notice?

Did you spot it? I didn't when I first saw it. I didn't see anything strange at all. Surely, it's obvious?

There are no women!

As late as 1970, the top five orchestras in the U.S. included fewer than five per cent women. It wasn't until 1980 that any of these top orchestras were comprised of 10 per cent female musicians.[29] By 1997, however, this percentage rose to 25 per cent. Today some are well into the 30 per cent bracket.

How did they do this? The size of a symphony or philharmonic orchestra is quite stable – they all have approximately between 75 and 100 musicians – so they haven't added new jobs to increase this percentage. They also haven't changed the jobs. For instance, there hasn't been a huge move towards harpists – traditionally played by women – or away from trombones, historically played more by men.

Orchestras simply realised they were suffering from an unconscious bias. It wasn't that people were deliberatly keeping women out. Everybody agreed women could play any instrument as well as men and were prepared to hire them: they just couldn't imagine a female trombonist in the same way as they could a male, for example.

They had been exposed to the pattern that had become ingrained in people's minds, of male musicians dominating orchestras.

It wasn't anyone's fault *per se*, but it was a hurdle for the women themselves.

However, it was identified as an issue that could be dealt with. In the 1970s and 80s, orchestras began holding blind auditions. Candidates were situated on a stage behind a screen to play for a jury that could not see them. In some orchestras, blind auditions are used just for the preliminary selection while others use it until a hiring decision is made.

CHAPTER 3 | 10
BEWARE THE PATTERN

This simple change made a huge difference to the number of women hired.

As the picture has now changed and the next generation of conductors and orchestra managers have been exposed to different patterns, blind auditions may no longer be needed.

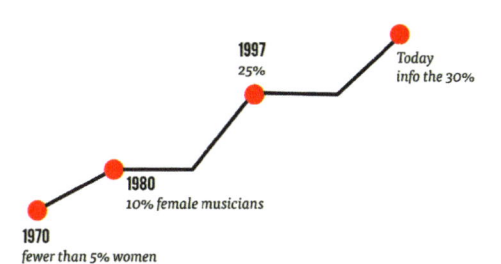

1970 — fewer than 5% women
1980 — 10% female musicians
1997 — 25%
Today — info the 30%

Our love of patterns is a BrainDrain

Patterns matter because our brains are lazy. Our brains use patterns as a shortcut when making decisions in ways we may not even be aware of. I certainly didn't notice the absence of women in the aforementioned orchestra picture and I even missed the fact that a graphic designer I was working with had not included any women in anything he produced for my company.

Clearly, *I'm* not deliberately biased towards women. This isn't about deliberate bias, and it's not about gender bias, but *it is* about HardTalk. I had an unconscious bias that I wasn't aware of (obviously). The problem with bias of any kind is that it's a 'Brain Drain': it makes your brain work against you in a HardTalk scenario, particularly if you're not aware of it.

There are lots of different kinds of bias, and we're all susceptible to any of them. Even if we don't want to be and even if we're 'good' people.

DIFFERENT KINDS OF BIAS

- A Queensland University study[30] found that blonde women earned, on average, seven per cent higher salaries than redheads and brunettes.

- A Duke University study[31] found that people with 'mature' faces experienced more career success than those with 'baby' faces. Baby faces were defined as those with small chins, wider cheeks, and bigger eyes, while mature faces were those with bigger chins, narrower facial features and smaller eyes.

- A Yale University study[32] discovered female scientists were not only more likely to hire male scientists, but they also paid them $4,000 more than female scientists.

It's unlikely the people in these studies actually wanted to pay blondes more money, enable people with mature faces to succeed at the expense of those with baby faces, or hire male scientists disproportionally and pay them more money.

Our unconscious biases are often so strong that they lead us to act in ways that are inconsistent with reason, as well as our values and beliefs.

Remember, it's not our fault. It's not your fault. It's just the way our brains work.

Also remember our brains are inherently lazy. They go for shortcuts: they're very clever like that. They don't just look for patterns, but patterns that repeat, and they use these to make 'decisions' (System 1 Homer Brain decisions).

It's not about our values. We can be absolutely

WORKHARD 64

committed to gender or race equality, for example, and still have biases. As we have seen, many studies repeatedly show that women feel bias towards women, people of colour towards other people of colour.

Your brain is not interested in value judgment – it's just looking for patterns. There are tests, supported by prestigious schools such as Harvard, where you can assess yourself for unconscious bias/pattern recognition.[33] It is absolutely eye-opening.

LEARN MORE AND TEST YOURSELF FOR UNCONSCIOUS BIAS VIA

www.hardtalk.info

Biases are believed to have played a role in financial crises, with bankers pursuing immediate gain while ignoring long-term risks and opposing information that didn't 'fit' with their assumptions. These bankers suffered from distance bias and confirmation bias.[34]

Biases affected administrations' ability to prepare and recover from natural disasters. Thanks to planning bias, people in Japan overestimated the degree to which they could control the negative effects of a tsunami, for example.[35]

All these biases, as well as many others, lead many a great company and institution to make disastrous and dysfunctional decisions.

But wait - companies and institutions don't make decisions, do they? Individuals and teams do. So why would we think bias doesn't affect us? Why would we think we are immune to the human brain's tendency to look for and use patterns?

We're not immune, bias does affect us, and becoming aware of that is the first step to preventing (unconscious) bias from blinding our judgement.

When a colleague pointed out the lack of female representation in the images we used internally and externally I was shocked, I hadn't noticed it myself.

I then started studying the subject of unconscious bias and hope that I would immediately notice a lack of women now. But I'm pretty sure I still have blind spots. So how can we deal with these?

COMMON BIASES THAT MAY AFFECT OUR ABILITY TO HAVE A SUCCESSFUL HARDTALK

Writing in Strategy+Business, social psychologist Heidi Grant Halvorson and Director of the NeuroLeadership Institute David Rock outlined the types of bias likely to be prevalent in organisations.[35] They identify 150 or so known common biases in five categories, based on their underlying cognitive nature: similarity, expedience, experience, distance, and safety. (They have named this the SEEDS model.)

❶ SIMILARITY

In-group Bias: Perceiving people who are similar to you (in ethnicity, religion, socio-economic status, profession, etc.) more positively. ("We can trust her; she comes from the same place as me.")

Out-group Bias: Perceiving people who are different from you more negatively. ("We can't trust him; look where he grew up.")

2 EXPEDIENCE

Belief Bias: Deciding whether an argument is strong or weak on the basis of whether you agree with its conclusion. ("This logic can't be right; it would lead us to make that investment I don't like.")

Confirmation Bias: Seeking and finding evidence that confirms your beliefs and ignoring evidence that does not. ("I trust only one news channel; it tells the truth about the political party I despise.")

Availability Bias: Making a decision based on the information that comes to mind most quickly, rather than on more objective evidence. ("I'm not worried about heart disease, but I live in fear of shark attacks because I saw one on the news.")

Anchoring Bias: Relying heavily on the first piece of information offered (the 'anchor') when considering a decision. ("First they offered to sell the car for $35,000. Now they're asking $30,000. It must be a good deal.")

Base Rate Fallacy: When judging how probable something is, ignoring the base rate (the overall rate of occurrence). ("I know that only a small percentage of start-ups succeed, but ours is a sure thing.")

Planning Fallacy: Underestimating how long it will take to complete a task, how much it will cost, and its risks, while overestimating its benefits. ("Trust me, we can finish this project in just three weeks.")

Representativeness Bias: Believing that something that is more representative is necessarily more prevalent. ("There may be more qualified programmers in the rest of the world, but we're staffing our software design group from Silicon Valley.")

Hot Hand Fallacy: Believing that someone who was successful in the past has a greater chance of achieving further success. ("Bernard Madoff has had an unbroken winning streak; I'm reinvesting.")

Halo Effect: Letting someone's positive qualities in one area influence overall perception of that individual. ("He may not know much about people, but he's a great engineer and a hard-working guy; let's put him in charge of the team.")

3 EXPERIENCE

Blind Spot: Identifying biases in other people but not in yourself. ("She always judges people much too harshly.")

False Consensus Effect: Overestimating the universality of your own beliefs, habits, and opinions. ("Of course I hate broccoli; doesn't everyone?")

Fundamental Attribution Error: Believing that your own errors or failures are due to external circumstances, but others' errors are due to intrinsic factors like character. ("I made a mistake because I was having a bad day; you made a mistake because you're not very smart.")

Hindsight Bias: Seeing past events as having been predictable in retrospect. ("I knew the financial crisis was coming.")

Illusion of Control: Overestimating your influence over external events. ("If I had just left the house a minute earlier, I wouldn't have gotten stuck at this traffic light.")

Illusion of Transparency: Overestimating the degree to which your mental state is accessible to others. ("Everyone in the room could see what I was thinking; I didn't have to say it.")

Egocentric Bias: Weighing information about yourself disproportionately in making judgements and decisions - for example, about communications strategies. ("There's no need for a discussion of these legal issues; I understood them easily.")

4 DISTANCE

Endowment Effect: Expecting others to pay more for something than you would pay yourself. ("This is sure to fetch thousands at the auction.")

Affective Forecasting: Judging your future emotional states based on how you feel now. ("I feel miserable about it, and I always will.")

Temporal Discounting: Placing less value on rewards as they move further into the future. ("They made a great offer, but they can't pay me for five weeks, so I'm going with someone else.")

5 SAFETY

Loss Aversion: Making a risk-averse choice if the expected outcome is positive, but making a risk-seeking choice to avoid negative outcomes. ("We have to take a chance and invest in this, or our competitors will beat us to it.")

Framing Effect: Basing a judgement on whether a decision is presented as a gain or as a loss, rather than on objective criteria. ("I hate this idea now I see our competitors walking away from it.")

Sunk Costs: Having a hard time giving up on something (a strategy, an employee, a process) after investing time, money or training, even though the investment can't be recovered. ("I'm not shutting this project down; we'd lose everything we've invested in it.")

This is a long list of biases, and throughout this chapter you'll discover definitions of various biases that might affect your ability to have HardTalk.

The bias blind spot

The problem is precisely that these biases are unconscious – we are literally unaware of them as they occur. It's very hard to just consciously 'watch out for biases', because there will never be anything to see. It would be like trying to 'watch out' for how much melanin your skin is producing.

Collectively, however, groups and organisations can become bias-aware in ways that individuals can't. Data can be collected, processes can be changed, and people can be held accountable if there's acceptance that it is needed.

Know your enemy

That said, there are always some ways in which you can start to prevent your biases unconsciously taking over by understanding more about them and where they come from.

1 Similarity biases

"People like me are better than others"

Most of us want to look good to others and feel good about ourselves. As a result, we want to perceive people who are like us as good too. This is fine insofar as it makes sure we want to protect and promote the people we feel are like us - our family, team, company. This bias goes deep.

According to some research[35], this tendency to categorise the world into *in-group* (people like me) and *out-group* (others) is so strong that just putting on different coloured tops results in greater liking for fellow members of the same team and less liking of members of another team. In addition, there is greater activity in several brain regions involved in emotions and decision-making (the amygdala, orbitofrontal cortex and striatum) in response to 'in-group' faces.

In other words, it's not that some people are "biased" and "bad" - this is just how our brains work. But this can also lead to us doing things we don't want to do, or not doing things we need to do.

Similarity biases affect many decisions involving people, including which clients to work with, what social networks to join and what contractors to hire. We are more likely to hire 'in-group' members, and, once we hire them, we're likely to give them bigger budgets, bigger raises and more promotions.

For example, a purchasing manager might prefer to buy from someone who grew up in his or her hometown, just because it "feels safer."

A board might grant a key role to someone who most looks the part, versus someone who can do the best job.

The bias is unfortunate because research (for example, by Katherine W Phillips) has shown that teams and groups made up of people with varying backgrounds and perspectives are more likely to make consistently better decisions and execute them more effectively, assuming everyone speaks up.[36]

It's also unfortunate in HardTalk because you might be more inclined to talk with people "like you", or to give them the benefit of the doubt because they are similar people.

To deal with similarity bias, find things in common with the out-group:

The best way to deal with similarity bias is to find things in common with the "out-group" and to focus on these, rather than on the things that are different, like race or gender or school attended.

When we look at the tips on changing processes later, we'll see examples of how to do this. You can never change your bias towards people like you, but you can make more people "feel" like you by looking at the things that are universal or that you share.

❷ *Expedience biases*

"If it feels right it must be true"

These kinds of biases are the mental shortcuts that help us make quick and efficient decisions. They're what System 1 (as seen in Daniel Kahneman's book "Thinking, Fast and Slow"[37]) relies on to get the right "feel". As we've seen, System 1 is where most of us like to be - it's easier, and a better experience.

Expedience biases tend to crop up in decisions that require just the opposite - coming to conclusions based on data, calculation, analysis and evaluation.

We see it with doctors who diagnose a tummy bug "because there has been a lot of it about recently," and miss the signs that would have been obvious at a different time. Or, with the consultant who has "seen this type of thing a hundred times" and so isn't listening attentively enough to find out what the client really needs.

> *We worked with a professional services firm who, like all such organisations, needed to improve their individual employee's ability to sell its services.*

> We told this group of highly capable, well-educated people that they would be taking part in a simulation during which they would meet with potential clients.
>
> They knew one or two salient facts about the client, such as an interest in real estate or international mergers.
>
> Despite telling us, before the exercise, exactly what behaviours they would want to see in others in this situation (i.e. asking open-ended questions, confirming and understanding) almost without exception they behaved just like the doctors and consultants mentioned previously - they immediately started to propose solutions.
>
> Not only did this annoy the potential client ("Who were they to give advice without understanding the situation?") but it also meant that a lot of information went uncovered, so opportunities were missed, and money was left on the table.

Inevitably, expedience biases tend to be worse when people are stressed - our brains try to put as much on "autopilot" as possible. It's our job to try to stop this and move back to System 2.

❸ Experience biases

"My perceptions are accurate"

Our brains have evolved to assume that what is perceived to be true is, in fact, true. We assume what we see is the truth, the whole truth and nothing but the truth, but, as seen in Chapter 2, our filters mean that we all interpret the 'truth' differently.

The problem is that if you are absolutely sure you are right, then the other person must be wrong, stupid, crazy or dishonest. Or something else which is unattractive.

We don't need to care about bad people. We don't need to listen to these people. So we don't need to have HardTalk.

This kind of bias is very hard to work against. The conviction your brain has created makes it difficult, even when you logically know that your perceptions are just a result of your filters.

On top of that, the *bias blind spot* means we can become convinced that we would notice any bias in ourselves. For example, "Look, I'm great at noticing it in others, so I must be good at spotting this stuff!"

❹ Distance biases

"Near is stronger than far"

One network in the brain registers all kinds of proximity - not just space and time, but also conceptual proximity, such as whether you own something or are related to someone. The closer an object, an individual, or an outcome is in space, time, or perceived ownership, the greater the value assigned to it and vice versa. Temporal discounting means that we are likely to choose the less but more immediate amount if offered USD 100 today and USD 150 in three months which, assuming there are no crazy levels of inflation, makes little sense as that's a guaranteed 50 per cent return in three months - something you'd imagine we'd like!

But distance bias contributes to a tendency towards short-term thinking instead of long-term investment. It can also lead us to neglect people or projects that aren't in our own backyard - a particular problem when we're in complex organisations and situations, and need everyone working across all silos and platforms and across different locations.

Framing can help with pattern blindness

To mitigate this kind of distance bias, use a skill we learned in Chapter 1 and frame the decision in such a way as to take distance out of the equation. We evaluate the outcome or object as if it were closer to us in space, time, or ownership.

Now, of course, it may be that time, space and ownership are important factors to consider and you should do so. Remember, while interest rates, or a sense of loyalty, or cultural proximity may all be great criteria to use when making a decision, you need to be aware that you're using them.

This part of HardTalk is all about getting back control of your brain – or giving control to the Spock Brain.

Set criteria before making a decision about something close to you or others

When we are close to something, we can make or fight for decisions that are not, in fact, in our best interest.

We saw this recently when a team we were working with was trying to decide which market to enter. Budgets had been reduced and what had previously been on the table was now no longer an option. The seven people on the team tasked with making and implementing a decision went around in circles for a long time and it became clear that there had been some major politicking before the meeting even started.

Tempers started to rise as individuals hardened their positions and descended into point-scoring and, in some cases, personal attacks

unlikely to strengthen team spirit. We stopped the fracas and asked the team to focus on building a list of criteria against which they could judge possible solutions,rather than first thinking about the solutions. This allowed them to stay focused on what really mattered to them.

5 *Safety biases*

"Bad is stronger than good"

The fact that we react more strongly to losses than to gains is a safety bias. This loss aversion makes sense if we consider that we evolved this way and our predecessors were the ones who responded quickly to a threat by running away, rather than the ones who thought "Hmmm, interesting rattling noise coming from under that stone. I'm sure it'll be something delicious we can eat and I'll be a hero".

Safety biases can influence any decision about the probability of risk or return, or the allocation of resources including money, time, and people.

These biases affect financial decisions, resource allocation and strategy development or planning for strategy execution, to name a few. Examples include not being able to let go of a business unit because of resources already invested in the project, and not being willing to innovate in a new direction because it would compete with the company's existing business (for example, Kodak back in the bad old days![38]).

Safety biases can change our decisions if those decisions are about risk/return or the allocation of any resources. In other words, the work of leaders and many managers, not to mention empowered individual contributors.

The problem is that safety biases can stop us having HardTalk, as we focus on what could go wrong, rather than what could **go right**.

Perhaps you're thinking that this isn't true for you - that you're interested in winning - and you're right. We all want to win, but most of us - probably including you - are more influenced by wanting to avoid losing.

This is why framing works.

If we present an opportunity as a gain, we focus people (and ourselves) on the risks involved. However, if the same decision is framed as a way to avoid a loss, people are more likely to ignore or justify the risk - even if the information is the same.

Exercise:
In your HardTalk scenario, what losses could you avoid if it went well?

> We like patterns and use them whenever we can, because we're lazy. We can make that work for us. For example, employers like Google help people control their weight by stacking smaller plates in front of big ones, and telling staff that research shows we tend to eat everything on our plate.[39]

So you think you know what's going on?

Now we're going to look in more detail at a few specific forms of bias and how they impact HardTalk, as well as how you can combat them.

The first of these is called the "False Consensus" bias - this makes us think we know what's going on, so we rush to solutions, don't listen and miss out on good ideas. This is part of what makes the ListenHard aspect of HardTalk so challenging.

For example, if you prefer vanilla to chocolate ice cream, you are likely to think most people have the same preference. People who prefer chocolate, however, will also assume they are in the majority. In an organisational setting, this assumption can lead to unnecessary conflicts, especially if leaders assume that many others agree with their preferences and make decisions accordingly.

On a sales call, you might not realise that other people are less excited by your product than you are.

When making a presentation, you might forget that others do not know the context.

If you are a senior leader pushing for a major organisational change, you might not see that others don't agree, or that they have legitimate concerns. None of these things make it more likely that you'll have successful HardTalk or that you'll be heard and will hear others.

Another kind of bias that can affect us is the "Golem Effect". This is where we convince ourselves that, because of something that happened in the past, we are right to now have low expectations.

In HardTalk scenarios, you most often see this when people just can't assume good intentions in the other party, so refuse to even try to fix the situation. We're not saying everybody is sweetness and light, but most people aren't evil. Even if they were, we still need to understand them, as we'll see later.

Our final bias is the "Halo Effect", where a single personality trait skews the general perception of a colleague's performance. The halo effect occurs when someone creates a strong first impression and that impression sticks. An example might be because somebody is famous they're considered to be right all the time.

How might the Halo Effect work against HardTalk? Well, you might hear people deciding against HardTalk because the guy is "nice" or "kind" or "hits his numbers".

These may all be right, but you might also be under the influence of the "Halo Effect". Facebook is very aware of the "Halo Effect". Its iconic logo stands in front of the logo of the previous owners of its headquarters building, to remind Facebook employees to watch out for the tendency to think that because the company is successful, there aren't any problems that could bring it down. That previous logo was Sun MicroSystems, the renowned IT company that failed.[40]

Exercise:
Bias: Golem, False Consensus and Halo

If you're worried your HardTalk partner might be a "Golem", then write down five things about what your HardTalk partner does, or is, that you can admire.

This can include things you've heard about.

If you think you might be assuming a False Consensus, get more data. Think of 10 questions you could ask your HardTalk partner. Imagine they are somebody else. Remember to use questions that start with Who, What, Where, When, Why and How.

If you suspect the Halo Effect is at play in your HardTalk scenario, ask yourself what other information you might consider if somebody else (other than your current HardTalk partner) was involved.

Bias affects us all at different times, in different ways

The regional GM of a multinational had recently hired a new marketing guy, excuse me, a marketing "guru". This new marketing director was the real deal, with a great track record of getting the job done. A few months in, and he'd already made things happen.

Unfortunately, some of the things he'd made happen weren't exactly part of the job description. Although he hit every one of his KPIs, and was fulfilling his job description, there were some troubling signs: almost half of his direct reports had left, and he was having trouble with the people he'd hired.

On top of this, he had started what amounted to a war with the compliance function. The GM was aware of the prevailing opinion that this guy didn't play nicely with others, and that he was prepared to do things usually considered out of bounds in this corporate culture. But the GM was too focused on the marketing director's ability to get things done to make the difficult decision to fire him: the Halo Effect was in full swing.

Ultimately, the marketing guru decided to leave, and the GM was left with lots to clean up, including a diminished reputation amongst his colleagues as he was considered too "weak" to deal with a difficult character.

Please note: we're not saying our biases are always wrong. Sometimes correlation does imply causation, and sometimes the boss, colleague or direct report really is a Golem, or should be wearing a halo - but it's rare. As always, self-awareness is the first step - noticing when you're potentially relying on System 1, then using the tools we looked at previously, as well as those coming up in the book, to return to System 2, so Spock is in control, and can focus on getting the results you want, while Homer takes a nap.

Patterns are great: they speed things up and show that we're learning. We all have bias - all of us - and for good reason.

Overall, biases are helpful and adaptive.

They enable people to make quick, efficient judgments and decisions with minimal cognitive effort. But they can also blind a person to new information, or inhibit someone from considering valuable options when making an important decision.

All the mitigation strategies or tools described here engage the brain's ventrolateral pre-frontal cortex, which acts like a braking system, helping you exercise cognitive control and broaden your attention beyond your own, self-specific viewpoint.

When thinking about how to manage our brains' tendency to like patterns and so be vulnerable to bias, there are four principles to bear in mind:

- Bias is universal. There is a general human predisposition to make fast and efficient judgements, and you are just as susceptible to this as anyone else. If you believe you are less biased than other people, that's probably a bad sign, and you may be more in need of help than most

- It is difficult to manage for bias in the moment you're making a decision. You need to design practices and processes in advance. Consciously identify situations in which more deliberative thought and strategies would be helpful and then set up the necessary conversations and other mechanisms for mitigating bias

- In designing bias-countering processes and practices, encourage those that place a premium on cognitive effort over intuition or gut instinct

- Individual cognitive effort is not enough (it's necessary but not sufficient). You must cultivate an organisation-wide culture in which people continually remind one another that the brain's default setting is egocentric. Remind each other that you will sometimes get stuck in a belief that our experience and perception of reality is the only objective truth, and that better decisions will come from stepping back to seek out a wider variety of perspectives and views

Bearing these tips in mind, here are some more you might find helpful when considering how you can mitigate your tendency (and that of others) to rely on unhelpful shortcuts, specifically in HardTalk scenarios:

❶ *Change processes - remember the orchestra?*

They changed the outcome by changing the process - which allowed them to be more objective.

Some of the big four consultancy firms (Deloitte, PwC, EY and KPMG) no longer share details of which university job applicants attended, to avoid bias.[41]

What process could you change to make HardTalk easier? To make it more likely you see the other person as complicated, with lots of different filters?

For example, one issue is how do you ensure people are heard - whether face-to-face or in writing? Implementing a brainstorming process, coming next, is one such process that enables easier HardTalk.

For whatever reason, it has been harder for women and minorities to get "air space" and, whether you believe it or not, this remains the case. It's not about whether you believe it to be true - the data is overwhelming. A few minutes on the internet will make it clear, if you need further convincing.

It's also not about fault.

I don't care if you, personally, have never done anything to shut down another human being. It's about you getting better results from hearing more diverse opinions and building a world where this is likely.

We need to put processes in place designed to make sure everyone is heard, and that everyone is more likely to hear.

BRAINSTORMING PROCESS

Brainstorming can be a great way to pool ideas and generate new ones. But not everyone enjoys the process. It's possible you might miss out on some great ideas - so why not change it? Instead of having everyone in a room shouting their ideas, impose a process that means everyone will be heard and everyone can hear.

1. Circulate the question or topic before you start. This allows people to come prepared with several creative options - and not feel stampeded by those comfortable just *"winging it"*. You might allow people to pool ideas anonymously before meeting face-to-face.

2. Keep the following guidelines in a place everyone can see during the brainstorm:
    - *One idea at a time - maybe taken from the pool of written ideas generated earlier*
    - *Build on the ideas of others*

3. Defer judgement (no criticism)

4. Stay on topic. The goal at this stage is to remix and add to others' ideas - not filter or critique. Thus, the default mode for a successful brainstorm is "yes, and..." (as in comedy improvisation)

5. Start and go around the room. Each person gives one idea at a time. No one gets skipped over, and no one should opt out.

6. Aim for a specific quantity of ideas. Let the group know the goal at the start, and don't stop until you get to that number.

7. Write and number each idea as it's generated. This helps people feel like they've accomplished something

8. Don't take a position on any idea. Consciously or subconsciously, others will take a cue from your lead. You want everyone in the room to feel heard, to have permission to speak their piece and to defer judgement during the brainstorm. Don't attach people's names to ideas, treat them all the same

If you really can't find enough time *(note: just 10 minutes is fine)* then you can tape a large piece of paper to a wall, write your question at the top and include a pen that people can use to anonymously write in their answers. Leave it up for a given period, then take a picture and transcribe it. While not providing all the advantages of the process suggested above, this method does remove some of the disadvantages of just asking for people's opinions.

Alternatively, you might use one of the many apps available for brainstorming, but before you do, make sure they incorporate the principles here.

② Hire widely and listen carefully

People can't be heard if they're not there in the first place. You'll need to hire widely. This will mean, for most of us, deliberately expanding our network outside people like ourselves in some way and making sure that hiring processes are as neutral as possible by introducing the equivalent of the orchestra's "blindfold auditions".

For example, when making recommendations, pepper the documents with references to the ways in which someone is "one of us." Have more than one woman on the short list so she's not the "odd one out".

With people already hired, put in place a process that makes it impossible for you to avoid a conversation *(for example, by scheduling monthly one-to-ones)*, and making a public commitment to doing so.

You could back this up by making it part of your, and your team's, KPIs. Add other KPIs designed to keep you aware of, and working against, pattern blindness or unconscious bias.

For example, you might have a target for "outsider" hiring to make sure you get a dose of external reality or commit to having someone observe team interactions.

Some clients have it as part of their KPIs to conduct a certain number of focus groups every year to get "real" information from their customers.

Connected to the idea of KPIs, but not limited to just financial reward, is the idea of changing what you reward.

Katharine Birbalsingh[42], founder of the Michaela Community School in the UK, and (full disclosure) a friend of mine, is creating an organisational culture around HardTalk, similar to that built by Facebook. She encourages HardTalk, and makes it explicit that it's expected if you want to be a success.

This is done in many ways including emails from her, as the boss, saying "When was the last time you had a candid or hard conversation?" and prominently displaying a sheet with stars for those who've done the right thing (it is a school!).

③ Flip it to test it

Unconscious bias is relatively easy to look at during the big moments, such as hiring and firing, but it's the day-to-day little things that lead up to those decisions that can be trickier.

CHAPTER **3** | 10
BEWARE THE PATTERN

When making routine decisions, like distributing work, allocating projects or deciding what to say in a HardTalk scenario, "flip it to test it". In other words, follow the advice of Kristen Pressner during her TED Talk[43] on bias. Ask yourself if you'd behave the same way, be worried about the same things, or come to the same Potentials if your HardTalk partner were different.

④ Use a checklist

Finally, we know a model or checklist can force System 2 to get into gear when System 1 just wants to do the easy thing. They're widely used in medicine and in airports for this reason.

We've created a HardTalk process - the Decision Tree – (downloadable via hardtalk.info) to help us stop, for example, making decisions on HardTalk based on our fear of bad results.

⑤ Add distance

Even if you can't change or influence processes in your workplace, you can use some of these tools to fight your own personal tendency to rely on Homer rather than Spock. For example, you can create distance by imagining you are giving advice to someone in your shoes rather than making the decision for your own enterprise. When making decisions for others, you can be less biased because the threat network is not as strongly activated.

Or imagine the decision has been already been made, and you are seeing it from a later point in time, evaluating it from there. Studies suggest that recasting events this way, from a more objective, distanced perspective, makes those events less emotional and less tied to the self.

Exercise:
What advice would you give someone facing your HardTalk scenario?

_____
_____
_____
_____
_____
_____
_____
_____
_____
_____
_____
_____
_____
_____
_____
_____
_____
_____
_____
_____

⑥ Get more data

Data can be used to track bias (or its effects), and to combat it.

Google uses huge amounts of data when hiring and promoting, deliberately to avoid bias.[44]

When thinking about a HardTalk scenario, force yourself to think about the bigger data set – and not just to focus on the Truths that lead you to the Potentials your brain likes because it's easy.

In particular, try to get data from other people who are unlike you in one way or another.

WORKHARD 76

If you think bias doesn't exist because you haven't experienced its effects, then congratulations! But if you can't hear people telling you it's happening to them then you need to really focus on the ListenHard part of HardTalk!

It is possible to be more like Spock than Homer. Or, in other words, to be more like we *imagine* we are when making decisions. But getting to System 2 is hard work because it takes effort, and we are set up for the easy option.

We're set up to go to System 1 whenever possible. When we are under stress – as in a HardTalk scenario, we are likely to be engaging our System 1 brains. That puts us onto automatic pilot just when we need to be in full control. We're not quite Pavlov's dogs, but we're not far off!

It's not about values or letting the other person off the hook. Rather, it's about combating our biases and making sure we see the whole story, so we have more control over our emotions, behaviour, and decisions.

We need this control because we can only control ourselves - we certainly can't control the next important factor in any HardTalk scenario: the other person!

CHAPTER 3 | 10
BEWARE THE PATTERN

CHAPTER SUMMARY 3

- *"We each contain System 1 thinking (The Homer Brain) and System 2 thinking (The Spock Brain); System 1 loves patterns and makes quick decisions with little information. System 2 is more logical, the executive brain that takes time to make decisions, evaluating the potential outcomes"*

- *"Our natural instinct to adhere to patterns makes us even more susceptible to biases in our organisations and the way we communicate. Many of them are unconscious, but the more we are aware of them the better prepared we are to overcome them"*

- *"The most common biases fault into 5 categories (SEEDS) Similarity, Expedience, Experience, Distance and Safety"*

- *"There are several ways your organisation can work to prevent biases holding your company back, through procedures and policies"*

CONSIDER THE OTHER

CHAPTER 4

Understanding the other person is crucial to knowing how to make sure you are correctly interpreted. Do to this you need to build empathy, trust and understanding in a quick and ethical way.

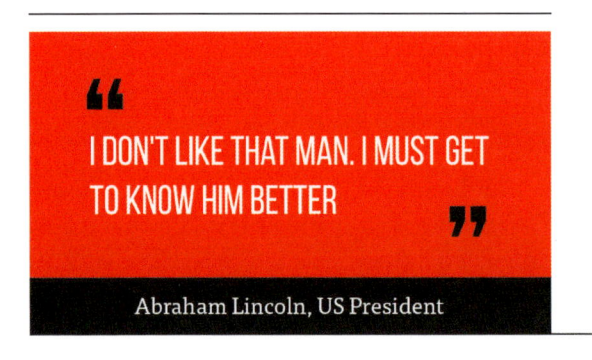

> " I DON'T LIKE THAT MAN. I MUST GET TO KNOW HIM BETTER "
>
> Abraham Lincoln, US President

PEOPLE ARE MYSTERIOUS BUT MAKE SENSE TO THEMSELVES (MOSTLY)

People are mysterious. It's hard enough to know what's going on in our own heads, never mind trying to understand others. We know this, and see it reflected in age-old proverbs like *"You can't judge a book by its cover"* or *"Still waters run deep"*.

Many of us - from behavioural economists to policemen - spend our lives trying to work other people out. And if you've ever been in a romantic relationship, you'll know just why those who get it right more often than not are revered and rewarded.

No matter how difficult it is, we need to understand people, if we're to understand how they climbed the Ladder of Action to the behaviour we're currently seeing. We particularly need to understand how they got there if we want to *change* that behaviour.

CHAPTER 4 | 10
CONSIDER THE OTHER

5 ACTION
4 EMOTION
3 POTENTIAL
2 FILTER
1 TRUTH

The more we understand other people and the impact we have on them, the more we can change the choices we make and have the impact we want.

Process of Progress

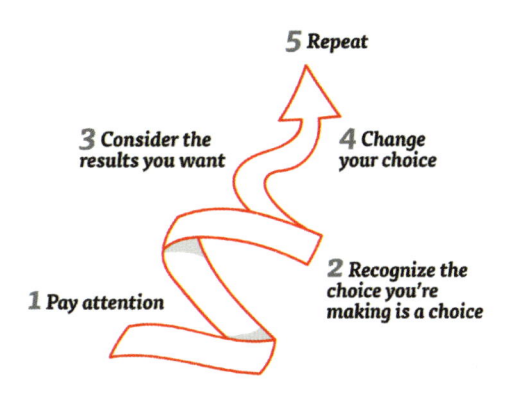

5 Repeat
3 Consider the results you want
4 Change your choice
1 Pay attention
2 Recognize the choice you're making is a choice

As we've already discussed, everything we see is interpreted through our own unique set of filters – who we are, the experiences we've had. That interpretation, or Potential, leads us to feel an emotion. The emotion then leads to us taking a course of action and feeling totally justified in doing so, whether or not it actually works in our favour.

To avoid allowing our action (our behaviour) to be led by our emotions we must manage these emotions. This doesn't mean we give them up or assume that they're wrong - it just means responding with curiosity.

When we see behaviour that isn't "right" or doesn't fit, we need to be curious about the cause, remembering that, just like us, other people react in a way that makes sense to them. Their filters are also sifting everything they see and hear - every Truth - and coming up with Potentials that are leading to their emotions and behaviour.

If we want to communicate effectively, to negotiate, to influence them, then we need to take this into account.

Imagine how easy life would be if you could really understand how another person sees the world. How they feel? Wouldn't it be easier to persuade them? To convince? To empathise? To come up with solutions they'd like and actually implement? To choose the right words at the right time?

Understanding the other person is key to knowing how to make sure that you are correctly interpreted. So how do we do that?

Listening is, of course, the most fundamental skill here, and we'll look at that in more detail later. But as we get ready to speak, we need to know how to build empathy, trust and understanding quickly and ethically, before we ever open our mouths.

We're still in the WorkHard phase of HardTalk, where we're getting our heads straight and doing the cognitive work needed to approach HardTalk scenarios effectively.

In this chapter, we'll look at empathy and understanding, and in the next, we'll consider trust.

YOU'VE GOT TO CONSIDER THE OTHER IF YOU WANT RESULTS

A lot of HardTalk scenarios involve one person or group trying to persuade another of the merits of a particular point of view or decision.

WORKHARD 80

A lot of time is wasted.

This is because the people doing the persuading present the "argument" in a way that would persuade them. They don't think about the filters of the other person.

If you really want to get your point across effectively, you need to understand, in a very clear and deep way, what the person currently thinks and feels (remember, it's emotions that lead to behaviour), and what they would need to hear and see to think and feel as you'd like them to.

> *You've got to consider the other if you want results.*

You've got to build empathy. This is both easy *and* difficult to do. None of the behaviours themselves are difficult, but you must remember to do them.

We already do it, to some extent, naturally: if you were born "neurotypical" i.e. in this case without any disorders that affect the way your brain deals with social interaction you have developed a *"theory of mind"*.[45]

The "theory of mind" is what psychologists call the ability to attribute thoughts and beliefs to others. Particularly when those thoughts and beliefs are different from ours. It's what allows us to understand what it means when we get a certain look from our partner or see particular body language. It seems to begin to develop at around the age of three and grow stronger over time.

The Spider in the Smarties Box[46] - a test for theory of mind

The Spider in the Smarties box is a test that has been developed by researchers to measure a child's ability to understand "false belief". False belief - or the understanding that another person's belief is different from reality - is measured by showing a child a box of chocolate Smarties with a toy spider inside and then asking the child what they think another person will think is inside the box. If the child is above the age of four and developing typically they will immediately understand that there is an opportunity for a joke as the other person will be confronted with eight hairy legs, instead of the anticipated coloured candy.

A recent study[47] found a link between theory of mind and increased connectivity between two brain regions: the temporoparietal junction, which is involved in thinking about others, and the inferior frontal gyrus, a region in the frontal lobe which supports thinking about abstract concepts such as belief and reality. As these connections become stronger, so, too, does our ability to empathise, pick up non-verbal cues, and realise that other people see things differently from us.

We all (assuming neurotypicality) have the ability to understand others. The behaviours aren't hard and our brains are set up to want to do it. Yet so often we fail. Some of this is down to other things our brains like *(such as the patterns we saw in Chapter 3)*, and some of it is down to the neurochemical soup swirling around.

The techniques aren't hard - they basically consist of the listening skills you already know and we will discuss more later, and trying to imagine the world through others' eyes. We have two skills for that. Neither are complicated and are intuitively the right thing to do - but common sense isn't always common!

CHAPTER 4 | 10
CONSIDER THE OTHER

1 PUT YOURSELF IN THEIR SHOES

Exercise:
What Truths might your HardTalk partner see? How might they interpret all the Truths in your HardTalk scenario?

This is an advanced version of the "fly-on-the-wall" technique we covered earlier. Get even more perspective by using the same technique to think about how the other person/people in your HardTalk scenario might be interpreting the Truths - to identify their Potentials and any Truths you might have missed. Write your thoughts here:

_____
_____
_____
_____
_____
_____

2 GET (HUMANISING) DATA

Learn more about the other person. Once you find out personal details about another person, you're more likely to find things you have in common and so kick-start the "similarity bias" we learned about earlier. It can be something as simple as realising that you both support the same football team, or have an ailing parent, that allows you to see them differently.

Humanising other people makes you less likely to fail in negotiation, according to research that shows indulging in stereotypes is the most common mistake in cross-cultural negotiation.

Follow people on LinkedIn or Twitter, read things they write, ask others about them. Try to find something that makes them "real" to you and that helps you understand their filters *(see the Trust exercise in Chapter 5).*

WHY IS SHOWING EMPATHY SO HARD?

Empathy is something we want, need and can do. It's relatively easy and brings great results. Professional negotiators rely on it to clinch deals and, in the case of law enforcement, save lives - so why don't we do it?

When we ask this question, we get a number of replies. People tell us they are:

A *Worried about appearing to agree with the other person*

Empathy does not mean sympathy - it doesn't mean you condone a particular belief or action or emotion or thought. It just means that you are trying to understand - really understand - why that belief, action, emotion or thought makes sense to your HardTalk partner. If you spend more time trying to build empathy - to see the world through their eyes - you will understand them better and so get better results.

For example, when an FBI hostage negotiator tells the hostage-takers that he understands their frustration, he's not implying he believes their actions are correct.

B *Worried the other person might say the "wrong" thing*

Sometimes we're so worried about what the other person might say in a HardTalk scenario that we don't give them a chance to speak at all. After all, if we don't ask any questions, we can't find out uncomfortable information or be challenged. Of course, pretending there isn't an elephant in the room doesn't mean you won't be overwhelmed with the smell of elephant poo. You want them to speak up because you want to make the best decisions you can and to discover all the possible obstacles to implementation.

C Worried about getting their message across

Obviously, our own ideas are always correct, and if other people could see the world in the same way we do, things would be great, right?

Well, no. Not really.

Actually, chances are that if we could see the world as others do, we'd be a lot more effective; we'd understand where they are coming from and what levers we're pressing and which ones we're neglecting.

Ironically, if we want to persuade, we must allow for the possibility of *being* persuaded and actively seek to understand. Because we (just like everyone else) need to hear and be heard.

3 STAY FOCUSED ON RESULTS AND KNOW WHAT'S OF VALUE

One way our brains can play with us is by invoking the law of reciprocity.

Reciprocity is a very common social norm which says that if I give something to you or help you in any way, you are then obliged to return the favour.

Reciprocity is used in lots of different ways. We see it used when charities and companies offer us something for "free and with no obligation". There is no legal obligation, but human beings work under norms, and it's a very well-established norm that we respond in kind.

Reciprocity can lead to us giving away things that are valuable, or treating as valuable things that are, in reality, worthless to us. When someone does something "good" for us, we want to do something nice for them in return. This can be dangerous if it confuses us about what's really of value in the scenario.

We worked with a lady (we'll call her Dania) who was a great negotiator. In fact, a large part of her job was to negotiate with suppliers (including us!) and she was a true professional. However, when it came to negotiating for herself her skills seemed to desert her.

> *Dania's boss was a very nice man. He had five children and was very understanding when Dania needed to work from home or start a little later because of her own child, who suffered from a chronic illness. Of course, Dania made up for any time she missed, and, in fact, she probably worked harder and more effectively than most of her colleagues as the constant time-pressure forced her to be focused and efficient.*
>
> *When it came to the yearly salary negotiation Dania allowed her bosses' flexibility and reasonable approach to invoke the reciprocity norm and she found herself walking away with 10 per cent less than colleagues who had achieved less and were not considered high-potential. When challenged, Dania explained that her boss had formalised her flexible working hours and she felt obligated to "play nice" in return. She even argued that she felt the flexible time she had already been given for free could be valued at about the same.'*

Exercise:
Your HardTalk scenario: what do you consider valuable?

What do you consider valuable? What might the other party in your HardTalk scenario value? Think beyond money. Information? Praise? The benefit of the doubt?

CHAPTER 4 | 10
CONSIDER THE OTHER

Convenience? Introductions? Sense of self-worth? Write your thoughts here:

_____
_____
_____
_____
_____
_____

So far, we've been envisaging scenarios in which our HardTalk partner is "nice" and gives us things we might, conceivably, want or that, at least, aren't something most people want to avoid. But what if that isn't the case?

What if the other person isn't "good"? What if what you receive is negativity or something else you perceive as "bad"? What if they turn up and their behaviour suggests that they are looking for someone to blame? What if they seem angry? What if reciprocity kicks in and you behave in the same way? Even when behaving like that stops you from getting the results you want?

The other person may not always be good! They might be acting in a certain way to get a reaction. We need, *(as we'll see in the next Chapter)*, to remember our purpose, and not allow reciprocity to change the way we need to turn up.

Exercise A: *Adjectives*
Your HardTalk scenario: how do you need to turn up?

We need to think about how we want people to describe us during this HardTalk - what adjectives can you use? Using adjectives here gives us the "tone" - they describe how you need your HardTalk partner to perceive you to get the results you want. Choose at least five adjectives (you can use the list below or find your own) and write them down in order of importance:

abrasive, abrupt, absent, absorbed, abusive, accessible, accomplished, accurate, active, adaptable, adventurous, aggressive, agreeable, alarmed, aloof, altruistic, ambitious, amused, angry, annoyed, anxious, arrogant, authentic, bewildered, bold, bored, brave, cagey, calculating, callous, calm, candid, careful, careless, caring, cautious, cheeky, cheerful, combative, compassionate, competent, complicated, composed, concerned, condescending, confused, considerate, courteous, cowardly, curious, decisive, defensive, defiant, demanding, dependable, determined, direct, discreet, easy-going, embarrassed, emotional, encouraging, enraged, enthusiastic, envious, ethical, evasive, exasperated, excited, extroverted, fascinated, firm, focused, forceful, formal, friendly, frightening, furtive, gentle, genuine, gloomy, gracious, grateful, guarded, guilty, heartfelt, helpful, hesitant, honest, honorable, humble, hurt, idealistic, ignorant, impolite, incompetent, inquisitive, insecure, instinctive, intelligent, interesting, irate, jealous, keen, kind, lazy, likable, loyal, mature, meek, miserable, mortified, naive, negative, nervous, observant, offensive, optimistic, panicky, penitent, perplexed, perceptive, polished, pompous, positive, powerful, prudent, qualified, realistic, reasonable, receptive, reflective, reliable, respectful, sarcastic, selfish, serious, shameless, shocked, showy, simple, sophisticated, stable, supportive, suspicious, sympathetic, threatening, trustworthy, unbiased, understanding, vacuous, vague, vengeful, watchful, weary, worried

_____
_____
_____
_____

Adjectives are Potentials. In other words, they're the result of how we (or others) see a Truth through our filters. This means that to be perceived in the way we want - to have our HardTalk partner see us as the adjectives we

WORKHARD   84

chose above - we need to consider their filters and then work out how we need to act.

For example, if you want to persuade an elderly Chinese bureaucrat that you are grateful and respectful, you might choose different actions to those you'd choose if you wanted a young American student to perceive you in the same way.

Exercise B: *Verbs*
Your HardTalk scenario: how do you need to turn up?

Go back to the Truths - what Truths do they need to see to get to the Potential you want?

We know how we want to be perceived. Now we have to get more specific. We move from adjectives to verbs. This is where you write down exactly what you need to do - such as listen, ask, clarify, complain, or maybe bow, to get the results you want. This moves us from the General (the adjectives) through the filters to the Specific (the verb) or the Truths. Write them down:

accuse, acknowledge, acquiesce, act, adjust, admit, admonish, advise, affirm, alert, announce, annoy, anticipate, apologise, appeal, appease, argue, ask, assert, assess, assist, avoid, backpedal, badger, badmouth, bargain, belittle, bemoan, betray, blame, broach, build, bully, categorise, challenge, charm, choose, clarify, coach, comfort, command, compare, compete, complain, comprehend, concede, conclude, condemn, condescend, confess, confront, connect, consider, consort, consult, contemplate, contend, contradict, convince, coordinate, correct, criticise, criticize, damage, debate, decide, decrease, defend, define, delegate, demand, demonstrate, denounce, deny, describe, detect, develop, differentiate, direct, disapprove, disclose, discourage, discuss, disguise, disparage, displace, dispute, disregard, distance, distract, disturb, divide, downplay, educate, elaborate, elevate, elude, empathise, empower, encourage, endorse, energize, enforce, engage, enthuse,

establish, evaluate, evoke, exaggerate, examine, exclude, excuse, exhibit, explain, explore, expose, fabricate, face, finalize, finish, fix, focus, forbid, force, frame, guide, hassle, hear, help, highlight, hinder, hold, humiliate, hurry, identify, ignore, illustrate, imagine, impede, imply, improve, include, influence, inform, insinuate, inspect, inspire, instruct, insult, interpret, interrogate, intervene, investigate, irritate, judge, justify, label, lament, lecture, listen, manage, manipulate, measure, mediate, mentor, mislead, mock, motivate, move, negotiate, normalize, notice, obey, object, oblige, observe, offend, offer, open, oppose, organize, outdo, outline, overcome, pass, patronize, persuade, placate, praise, pressure, pretend, prevent, promise, promote, provoke, pry, publicize, punish, push, qualify, question, raise, reason, reassure, reciprocate, recommend, reconsider, redirect, reflect, refocus, refuse, reiterate, reject, remind, repair, rephrase, replace, reply, reproach, request, rescind, rescue, research, resent, resist, resolve, respond, retreat, reveal, revise, revoke, reward, say, scrutinise, seek, settle, share, shout, show, sidestep, silence, simplify, snub, speak, specify, speculate, spy, stipulate, strengthen, stress, summarize, surprise, sympathize, tackle, teach, test, thank, theorize, trivialize, underestimate, understand, unite, upset, urge, validate, verify

_____
_____
_____
_____
_____
_____
_____
_____

If you're feeling like everything about HardTalk makes it nearly impossible for you to manage your own behaviour - never mind focusing on the other - then you're not alone. But it's the ability to do the latter that can make all the difference. Of course it's difficult - if it wasn't, everyone would do it and we wouldn't have called it HardTalk.

CHAPTER SUMMARY

- *"Understanding our HardTalk Partner and how they climbed their Ladder of Action is key to successful HardTalk. The more we understand people, the more we can get the results we want"*

- *"We build empathy best by putting ourselves in their shoes, learning more about the other person from people who know them, focusing on results and what is of value"*

- *"Don't worry about appearing to agree with them, about them saying the wrong thing or about not getting your message across – empathy won't cause any of these things to happen"*

- *"Determine what result you want and how valuable it is to you. Consider what adjectives would describe your behaviour and is it the best one to achieve your goal. What verb would describe your behaviour during your HardTalk and is it the best one to achieve your goal?"*

REMEMBER YOUR PURPOSE

CHAPTER 5

Your Purpose is what you really want in the long-term. Your perceived Purpose is what your behaviour suggests you want. You won't succeed if they stay separate..... get aligned.

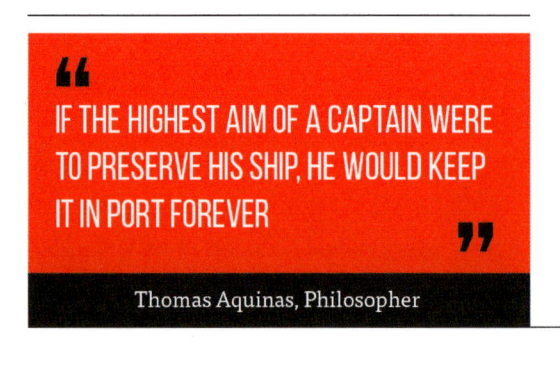

> "IF THE HIGHEST AIM OF A CAPTAIN WERE TO PRESERVE HIS SHIP, HE WOULD KEEP IT IN PORT FOREVER"
>
> Thomas Aquinas, Philosopher

WE ALL HAVE GOOD PURPOSES AND BAD PURPOSES

Imagine this: you get up in the morning and you have a perfectly lovely breakfast with your favourite people/book/device and on your way into work you remember you have a team meeting. The first item on the agenda is how one of the projects you work on is behind a few weeks. You've worked well with everyone on the team before; what kind of Purpose do you have?

I've asked this questions to thousands of people at this stage and the vast majority will come up with something positive and healthy. They might say to "understand" or "advise" or "interpret" or, even, "to console".

I then pose this scenario: Let's imagine a guy has just found out - on the first day of the working week, *(from his assistant just 10 minutes before a progress update meeting is due to start)* - that his team has fallen behind on a project that's close to his heart. He's new at the company and is keen to make his mark. What kind of Purpose might he have?

Pretty much universally the answers to this question are less positive and include Purposes such as "punish" or "blame" or "guilt" or "save face" or "to avoid recrimination".

Returning to the first scenario, what if it hadn't been such a great start to your day? Instead of a lovely breakfast with your favourite whatever, you woke up late because you missed the alarm? What if one or more of the others on

CHAPTER 5 | 10
REMEMBER YOUR PURPOSE

the team were irritating/had thrown you under a bus last week? What if one of them insulted you before the meeting began? In front of your boss?

What might your Purpose have been in the team meeting? Would that really match the results you want?

> "We are very good lawyers for our own mistakes but very good judges for the mistakes of others"
> — Anonymous

If you're honest (and normal!) you'll probably admit that your Purpose in that scenario might not be one that you'd be quite as happy sharing with others.

The chances are that in the meeting, in the moment, your Purpose will have changed.

It's no longer the long-term, healthy Purpose that gets us the long-term results we want - for ourselves, for others, for relationships. Instead it becomes a short-term Purpose that, if we achieve it, will make us feel good for a few minutes - but does nothing to get us what we really care about.

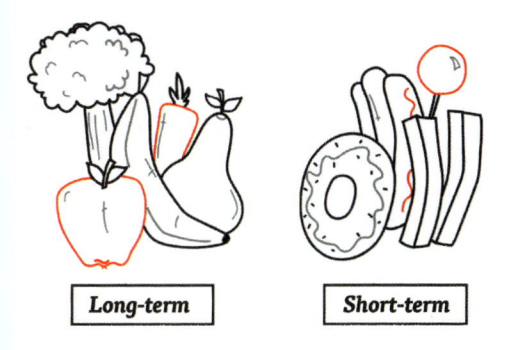

Long-term | Short-term

The problem is that, in a HardTalk scenario, we often behave in a way almost guaranteed to achieve any Purpose, other than the one we want. And worse, we feel great about it (for a while at least), because of the "Fundamental Attribution Bias."

FAB!
The Fundamental Attribution Bias-designed to make you feel good when you should be behaving well instead.

AT LEAST 2 A DAY

We tell ourselves other people's bad behaviour is based on their personality and motives, whereas our behaviour is a result of external circumstances. Other people are late because they're disorganised or disrespectful. I'm late because of the traffic. It's called the Fundamental Attribution Bias and it lets us get away with bad behaviour because it gives us an excuse.

The excuse is "well, the other person is "bad" and so I don't have to behave well - I can go speechless or squash them - it's the reasonable thing to do". My response to this is simple - stop thinking about what the other person "deserves" and think about what you deserve. What results do you want? That's what should dictate your behaviour!

The CFO was furious. One of his team members had made such an obvious mistake that he couldn't believe he'd missed it. Even worse, he hadn't spotted it before the budget meeting, and so had made a fool of himself in front of

WORKHARD 88

the whole management team and the various country heads. What on earth was going on? He'd been in this position for three years, and really thought the team was finally up to doing the job in the way he wanted - and now this?

He was despondent at the amount of time he'd wasted. He really believed in developing others, and had spent countless hours coaching and mentoring his team. Even when he knew they'd leave soon; even when they really should have been fired because they lacked the right skills; at the expense of his relationship, and time spent with his children. He enjoyed seeing people get better and finding pride in what they do - and he liked his team as people too.

He picked up the phone and asked his assistant to call the whole team for an emergency meeting. The CFO strode into a glass-walled meeting room in the middle of the open-plan office, sat down and said to his team: "We have a problem." One member of the young team, who had only been with the company for six months and was used to the relaxed, informal style her boss had been trying to make the norm, said: "We'd better call Houston" and, at that, the normally relatively mild-mannered CFO exploded.

"This is exactly the problem with you guys - you think everything is a joke! Well, it's not. Your incompetence has consequences and not just for you but for me. I'm fed up of being the only one who takes responsibility - it's no wonder I missed this given how many of your mistakes I pick up every day!" The team sat, silent as the CFO continued to shout for the next five minutes until he stopped, suddenly, saying "I've had enough of you all for today. Get back to work. We'll start again tomorrow."

What do you think the team felt was the CFO's Purpose in that meeting? Given his behaviour, what do you think they would have assumed his objectives were?

> What were his long-term objectives?
> How did his behaviour advance his long-term objectives?
> How do you think he justified his behaviour to himself?

HOW CAN YOU TELL SOMEONE'S PURPOSE?

The simple answer is you can't.

We can't see inside people's heads, so we extrapolate their Purpose from what we see them do and hear them say. In essence it's down to behaviour - what they say and what they do - and, of course, how we interpret this behaviour due to our own filters.

The problem is other people do that to us too, and because of the Fundamental Attribution Bias, they assume our behaviour is a result of our personality and motive or Purpose and not just because of, for example, a bad night's sleep, a cold cup of coffee or irritating news about a family member.

We might have a good Purpose in mind if asked in advance, but in the moment? Under stress? What would people think our Purpose is in HardTalk if all they have to go by is our behaviour?

Exercise:
Your HardTalk scenario...what's your Purpose?

What would someone/your HardTalk partner think your Purpose is in your HardTalk scenario if all they have to go by is your behaviour?

_____
_____
_____

CHAPTER 5 | 10
REMEMBER YOUR PURPOSE

Process of Progress

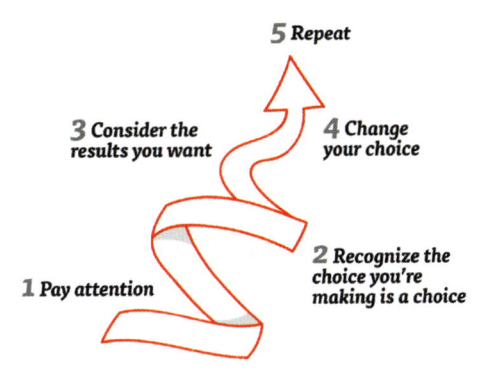

5 Repeat

3 Consider the results you want

4 Change your choice

1 Pay attention

2 Recognize the choice you're making is a choice

Your behaviour is all other people **do** have to go on. They can't see inside your mind, so will assume your behaviour is a choice that reflects your personality and your Purpose. Whether they're right or wrong doesn't matter. What they **perceive** is important.

We can have one of two kinds of Purposes – short and long-term – depending on whether Homer or Spock *(see Chapter 3)* is in charge.

You want people, usually, to know your good, long-term Purpose (although there may be some scenarios in which you want there to be ambiguity).

In other words, you want your behaviour to reflect Spock's considered approach and not Homer's "if it feels good right now let's do it". One way of doing that is by focusing on, as the Spice Girls famously sang: "What you really, really want".

If you can focus on that, it's likely your behaviour will reflect it. Yes, it's all about self-awareness and is as simple and as difficult as that. You have to be observing your behaviour and the impact it has on others.

For example, perhaps you want to be perceived as accessible - that's your Purpose and the Potential you want them to have. But then you realise the team you are working with interpret your behaviour as "too friendly for a boss". You can then change the choice you're making about how you turn up, so you are perceived as you want to be perceived.

A senior partner in a law firm turns to a new associate as they leave the first client meeting they've had together, sighs, and says "So I guess it's obvious Brian is your mentor." The new associate immediately reacted - his face tensed and he withdrew from further conversation. Earlier he had been engaged and had made some interesting points. The senior partner had recently taken a HardTalk programme and was ListeningHard. This meant she was able to notice and consider the change in behaviour and recognise it as abnormal.

She used skills we're going to learn in the upcoming ListenHard and SpeakSoft sections of the book to bring up the subject, and eventually learned that the associate was upset because he had heard rumours that his mentor

WORKHARD 90

wasn't universally valued amongst the senior staff. He interpreted the partner's Purpose as being to let him know that he'd under-performed and was being considered in the same light as the mentor.

In fact, the partner had known the new associate's mentor for many years and knew they are particularly bad at building associates' self-confidence. She had noticed the associate seemed nervous and his voice was trembling, and was considering the options available to help him. Her Purpose was not to censure but rather to develop the more junior people, and build the strength of her team. When she realised the confusion, she was able to use some of the skills we'll cover later in this chapter to make sure she was properly understood.

When the senior partner understood what the associate was upset about she was able to reassure him as to her real Purpose. And he believed her.

When I tell this story in front of groups this is where I lose them. There is often a sense of "yeah, sure, right, but back in the real world!" when they hear that the associate and the partner calmly worked out there had been a misunderstanding and moved on with a better relationship than before.

> Of course, when challenged, most of the same sceptics will acknowledge that they would, obviously, behave well - they're just surprised that others do. Why is that? Why do we feel like some people shouldn't be believed, and that most people won't believe us when we're prepared to believe others? How does it impact our ability to get the results we want?

Have a look at these HardTalk scenarios. How do you think they went?

1. A client sends a supplier an SMS saying "We need to talk. Call me now."

2. A group of people are meeting to discuss talent succession. One member says: "I don't understand why Mariya is still on this list of high potentials." Another member, Mariya's mentor, interrupts to say, "She has as much right as anyone else to be there - her numbers were extraordinary last year."

Neither of these conversations went well. In each case there was confusion around Purpose with people assuming a less than positive Purpose (remember - we're doom-mongers and so usually assume the worst) and becoming upset, nervous or annoyed.

What happened?

1. The supplier was nervous because she assumed the client was unhappy. She interpreted the client's Purpose as being to complain and so was defensive. In fact, the client did have a problem and was getting a lot of hassle from his boss, so he was calling to find out what was going on. His Purpose was to investigate and understand, not to complain and blame.

2. The mentor assumed the other team member was questioning Mariya's right to be there and pushed back strongly. But, in fact, the member was suggesting that Mariya already qualified to be on a **different** list with extra funding and more opportunities for access to senior people and stretch assignments.

The people starting these HardTalks would say their motive was, for example, to develop their team/to understand a problem/ to make sure the rules are followed, and yet they were misunderstood, and so their HardTalk became just that little bit harder.

Make it less likely you fall into the same trap by following these rules:

❶ Share your Purpose explicitly

Sometimes it seems we're so sure we'll be disbelieved that we don't even tell the other person what our Purpose is.

Tell the other person what your intention is. Don't leave any room for doubt. They might not believe you, but they also just might. Especially if you're telling the truth. It's worth a go surely?

As we'll see in the SpeakSoft chapter, sharing our Purpose at the beginning of the HardTalk can also help us to remember the ultimate Purpose: i.e. to hear and be heard.

To hear and to be heard

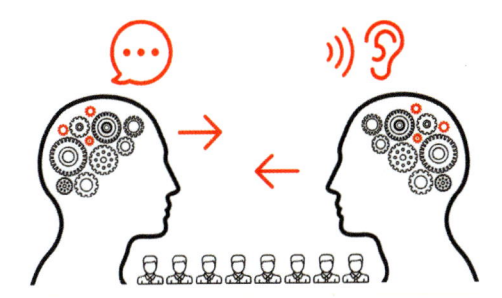

If you can't find a positive Purpose, then why are you are having a HardTalk at all?

Your ultimate Purpose is to hear and be heard. It's to share what you've noticed, and put forward a Potential and maybe some Consequences. It's to listen, so you can understand why something is the way it is, and work with the other person to make it better.

These are all reasonable things to want. So why not tell people? Why not say "I want to understand/decide/confirm/explain...?" Are you afraid you might be held accountable? That you might actually have to behave as though that's what you want?

❷ Be consistent

Inconsistency drives people crazy! Inconsistency between how you behave in one situation versus another will always raise alarm bells.

If you want to be believed when it counts you need to be consistent all the time in your behaviour, or have a clear explanation of why you are being inconsistent.

That may seem unreasonable when you look around and see others behaving inconsistently, but it's not about them right now. It's about you and the results you want.

Maybe we're so aware of our own inner inconsistencies that we struggle to understand that others are just judging us on our behaviour. We fail to understand how important it is that our behaviour is consistent with what we say our Purpose is.

Exercise:
Your HardTalk scenario...what's your Purpose?

What is your Purpose in having this HardTalk? Choose at least three verbs (from the list on page 85 or choose your own) that explain your Purpose.

Really? Does it match the results you wrote about on Page 89? If not, if there is inconsistency something needs to change.

Look back at the verbs you chose on page 85, in Chapter 4. Now, are you ok with behaving like that? If you do that, will it further the healthy long-term Purpose you identified?

If not, then you might have some more work to do.

Exercise:
Your HardTalk scenario: what's their Purpose?

Consider the filters of your HardTalk partner and their Truths, and ask yourself what their Purpose might be.

As we saw in the previous chapter the more we can "inhabit" our HardTalk partner the more likely we are to get to a successful outcome. So we need to think about what the other person's Purpose might be.

But how can you tell?

Again it's easy to get this wrong. It's their behaviour of course. But it's their behaviour read through our own filters. We assume that certain things - a certain way of dressing, a gesture or choice of vocabulary - tell us about somebody's Purpose. We also judge what their Purpose might be based on our experience with the individual(s) in front of us, or people who are like them in some way.

As we've seen, this is normal human behaviour - we look for shortcuts and patterns - so it's not exactly our fault. But the only way to find out someone's Purpose is to ListenHard and go back down the Ladder to Action to discover the Truths.

CHAPTER 5 | 10
REMEMBER YOUR PURPOSE

③ Contrast to make your Purpose clear.

Your perceived Purpose is what your behaviour suggests you want.

It's what others assume - based on what they see and hear through their filters, including their past experience with you - and it's what really matters. If you think your Purpose might be misconstrued, (why might it?), how can you deal with that?

Telling people what you do want is helpful, but telling them what you don't want is even better. This is called *contrasting*. And it's a great tool for reassuring our HardTalk partner as to our Purpose.

Contrasting is a game of two halves - with a Purpose in each.

I DON'T want to suggest that you're a liar.

I DON'T want to embarrass you in any way.

I DIDN'T want to imply that you're micromanaging.

I DO want to get to the bottom of where this money went.

I DO need to tell you something that I think will be useful information for you.

I DID want to let you know that you could have some time back if you need it.

In the first half, you tell your partner what you didn't or don't want to achieve in the conversations.

I didn't / don't want / don't mean to...

And in the second half you tell them what your Purpose is:

I did / do want / do mean to...

You can do this upfront, or in the moment:

a) "Upfront" Contrasting

If you're afraid the other person will misconstrue or misunderstand what you're doing, then let the other person know why you're having the conversation. "I don't mean to be rude" is not a contrast. Nor is "no disrespect", because they don't share a Purpose.

Sometimes you know the other person is likely to assume the worst Purpose possible. Maybe because you've told them to, or simply because you didn't tell them otherwise.

By "you've told them to" we mean you've previously given reason for your HardTalk Partner to doubt your Purpose, or to have reason to believe your Purpose is not a good one, focused on long-term results. If that's the case, you have to work to rebuild trust.

If your Purpose is good, and yet you think your Partner might, for whatever reason (for example because of the situation, your history or their experience), misunderstand or misconstrue what you want to say, you can use contrasting upfront. This means stating at, or near, the beginning of the HardTalk exactly what you do and don't want to achieve.

WORKHARD

EXAMPLE

Priya had recently joined a company as leader of a team of seven. One of her direct reports, Ahmed, had covered the role she had just taken on as an interim for three months. When the job was advertised, Ahmed was the only internal candidate who applied for the role. There were three other external candidates on the list, including Priya who got the job.

Priya left her old role as she felt she was still being treated like the intern she was when she joined her previous company eight years ago. She had been passed over on a number of promotions herself, so could easily relate to how Ahmed might feel about her in her new role, having taken the job he had done for three months.

But Ahmed wanted to help Priya. Disappointed and not necessarily averse to hearing about other options right now, he still wanted to see his colleagues and the organisation do well. He had listened to the feedback about his three months in the role, and saw some merit in what the interviewing panel had to say, although he disputed some of it too.

If you were Ahmed would you offer to help?

How might Priya misconstrue any offer of help from Ahmed'?

What is Ahmed's actual motive (his Purpose) for speaking up and offering help?

How could Ahmed use contrasting to make his Purpose clear?

It might sound like:

"I don't want to offer advice where it's not wanted, I do want you to know that I'm here to help when you need me"

"I don't want to imply you don't know how to do your job properly, I do want to let you know that I know how tough it is and I'm happy to help if I can."

Other examples of contrasting include…

"I don't want to imply that you're not doing your job properly, I do want to be absolutely sure that we've dotted every **i** and crossed every **t**"

"I don't want to put you on the spot, I do need to find out what happened in the meeting you attended yesterday."

Obviously, you don't want to suggest things that aren't true and are unlikely to have occurred to your HardTalk partner, and so Contrasting *upfront* may not be necessary.

It's still possible, however, that your HardTalk partner misunderstands your Purpose and you realise this only as you are talking. This is a chance to contrast *in the moment*.

b) "In the moment" Contrasting

Have you ever been completely surprised at the Purpose somebody has assumed you have? It's often quite an uncomfortable experience as you realise that their perceptions of you are far removed from the reality (as you see it), and what you hoped you put across.

FOR THE SAKE OF A NEEDLE….

A project team meeting degenerated into tense silences and occasional snide comments when team member, Iain, suggested his colleague, Keo, should: "Pay more attention to the detail of the contract with the lighting suppliers."

Keo reacted by saying:
"Hey, why don't you focus on your own business? The manuals are miles behind where they need be. Go and sort that out – you do your job and I'll do mine."

Iain immediately retorted: "What's your problem? I'm just trying to help!"

"I'll ask for your help when I need it" was the only reply.

Muttering, Iain shrugged, "I was just trying to warn you..."

After the meeting, both Iain and Keo spent time considering how to "manage" the other and built factions, over time affecting the outcome of the project, adding stress to the lives of all involved, and creating a negative impact on the bottom line. This affected their own job security and that of their colleagues.

This is a scenario we see played out again and again. And it can be solved by contrasting. The clue is in the phrase "I was just trying to..." If you hear yourself saying that in your head, then there's a chance to stop and make your reality clear, through contrasting.

In the example here, it might sound like: "I didn't want to suggest you need help, I did want to warn you about my previous experience with those suppliers."

or

"I wasn't trying to suggest that you didn't know your business, I wanted to let you know about a previous problem with the lighting suppliers."

You might also consider apologising if you feel it's appropriate, for example: "I'm sorry. I didn't mean to suggest you weren't taking your role seriously. I *did* want to address the fact that you've been late to the last three project meetings."

or

"I'm sorry. I didn't want to blame you for the mistake. I did want to find out why it happened, so we can fix the process."

NB: *You must address both sides i.e. what your Purpose is and what the other person might have misconstrued it to be.*

Exercise:
Your HardTalk scenario: Contrasting

What Contrasting could you use in your HardTalk scenario?

What might your HardTalk partner imagine your Purpose to be? Put yourself in their shoes - knowing what they know and only what they know - how might they see the world differently? Might the other person misunderstand or misconstrue your motives? How? Choose two verbs - one that does NOT explain your Purpose, but describes a possible other Purpose, and one that does. Write two contrasting sentences like the examples suggested earlier:

_____
_____
_____
_____
_____
_____
_____
_____
_____
_____
_____
_____
_____
_____
_____
_____

YOUR "NATURAL" BEHAVIOUR MAY NOT GET YOU WHAT YOU WANT

If your "natural" behaviour and your Purpose are out of line, what can you do?

You have to change your behaviour.

Some people worry that this means they need to change their personality. That's not the case. What we are talking about is having a suite of different behaviours you can use in different HardTalk situations when you want to be understood in a certain way, and to ListenHard to understand others.

Other times, we hear concerns that we're suggesting "tricking" people by behaving dishonestly.

That's not the case.

Rather, it's about getting them to understand what you really want, your real Purpose, and, sometimes, making sacrifices to do that.

A client we worked with was the most stereotypical straight-laced Englishman you can imagine. Brought up in a traditional "prep" school from the age of six, before moving to a good public* school, his emotional intelligence was, to put it mildly, underdeveloped, and he trusted no one. (We're not implying this is true of all public school pupils, but it was very true of him.)

He had risen up the corporate ladder as a result of his strong technical skills and now, having moved companies in his early 40s, found himself running a team of eight people. In his previous role, he had only had one direct report because his mentor knew he wasn't comfortable with "the people stuff" and had "protected" him from this aspect of skills development. Now CFO, he micromanaged, and his team were not reacting well. We were asked to work with the CFO and, eventually, his team, to help strengthen their performance.

This man's Purpose was clear from our first interview. He wanted to build a strong team that could meet aggressive targets without burning out and he needed to do it quickly. He knew he couldn't achieve his goals alone and he knew he was floundering because his instinctual behaviour was not getting him the results he wanted. We started by working on what helps a great team to get great results. His team was filled with technically competent people who come from a diverse backgrounds.

The first thing he learned was you need "safety first" if you want results (*based on findings from Google's Project Aristotle [48] and lots of work done by Patrick Lencioni.[49]*)

At first glance, this need for psychological safety can seem a bit soft as it says we need to "feel safe" if we are to be effective at HardTalk. Remember your ultimate Purpose is always to hear and be heard, and that means building Trust.

PROJECT ARISTOTLE

Google researched what qualities the most high-performing teams shared, and found it was their ability to both speak up and listen. In the best teams, everyone speaks up and for more or less the same amount of time. Further research shows that the thing that makes this possible - for people to really be candid and yet be respectful and build relationships - is vulnerability-based trust.[48]

*In the UK a "public" school refers to a fee-paying school.

If you don't have psychological safety or vulnerability-based trust then your Purpose is immaterial

We need to feel safe if we are to hear and be heard; if we want results. So let's talk about that Purpose - building safety. Because whatever other verbs you chose earlier to describe your Purpose, building safety comes before all of them.

When we don't feel safe, we don't speak up.

We need to speak up, because as commerce becomes increasingly global and complex, the bulk of modern work is more and more team-based. A study reported in Harvard Business Review, January 2015[50], found that "the time spent by managers and employees in collaborative activities has ballooned by 50 per cent or more" over the last two decades and that, at many companies, more than three-quarters of an employee's day is spent communicating with colleagues. This can, and should, lead to good things but too often it results in time wasted and morale sapped due to miscommunication and unnecessary politics.

We assume if we get clever people together in a room and pay them they will work together effectively. But they don't.

They need to feel safe if they're to speak up, and if we are to take advantage of the possibilities of this increased level of workplace collaboration. This takes work. It's not about "team building" once a year (although that has its place); it's about the day-to-day work, the behaviour you show every day that either supports or diminishes people who speak up.

Whatever action you choose, you're leading by example.

> *Psychological safety - a sense of confidence that the team will not embarrass, reject or punish someone for speaking up*

Psychological safety is the essential ingredient in high-performing individuals and teams. We need to feel safe if we are to work together effectively.

You have psychological safety in a team where there is interpersonal trust and mutual respect and where people are comfortable being themselves. It is based on vulnerability trust - which can be much harder to build than we think!

There are two kinds of trust.

COMMON TRUST

The confidence / belief that a co-worker or team member won't break generally accepted laws, norms, policies, etc.

This first kind is pretty easy to achieve. If you don't have that level of trust in your colleagues, get out now!

The second, however, is harder. It involves acknowledging that all of us are human beings and will screw up on occasion. It also means being humble enough to admit that we, like everyone else, are vulnerable.

VULNERABILITY-BASED TRUST

The belief you can do things like take risks, ask for help, admit mistakes, or confront and hold others accountable without fear of retaliation, humiliation or resentment.

Without this trust we're not going to speak up and we're not going to get the right result. Without trust, we "squash" others or go silent.

Speechless - staying quiet when you have something that should be heard

It's easy enough to understand why a lack of trust would make somebody go speechless.

If we believe we will be punished for speaking up, then of course it makes sense not to do so. Of course, we don't go entirely "speechless" as, although we're not using words, we're certainly communicating. It might be an eye-roll when they speak, a raised eyebrow on hearing an opinion, a whispered conversation that gets back to them. Whatever it is, we're not building any good relationships and not getting the results we want either.

If there's no trust, then we're certainly not going to risk having a HardTalk, and may not "let it go" so causing even more trouble and a toxic environment.

Squashing - not encouraging others to be heard

We all have the capacity, given the right situation and HardTalk partner, to find ourselves not just "Speechless" but a "Squasher".

Here, fear leads us to shut the other person down. The fear, remember, is a primal response - an overreaction and, when you remember this, it becomes easier to remember that everyone feels it. Even those who, it seems to you, have nothing to fear from you – i.e. those above you in the organisational hierarchy. They might fear how you can make them feel about themselves, for example. Or they might fear you're after their role.

How do Squashers behave?

At the worst end of the spectrum we use hierarchy or seniority or some other "weapon" to shut the other person up, by shouting, or threatening, for example.

At the other end of the spectrum, it's just people not paying enough attention - interrupting, not making eye contact, playing on their phone. Especially if they're leaders. If you show a lack of interest, then don't be surprised if people assume you're not interested.

CHAPTER 5 | 10
REMEMBER YOUR PURPOSE

Newly-appointed staff were due to join a company in the next few weeks, and had agreed to attend a special, extra session at a company off-site before everyone else turned up, to get them up to speed quickly.

We walked through the outcomes of the previous six months of working with the leadership team of this ambitious organisation, aware of the need for massive change to face new challenges in a demanding environment.

The group of new staff digested the newly-agreed vision and mission, key policies and procedures, as well as the behavioural framework and a number of other things, clarifying and answering questions along the way. They were joined by a few others who had missed earlier work, and they then completed a team exercise.

This particular team exercise involved discussing what to do in a survival scenario. The idea is that individuals first answer questions, then the team discusses, and they reach a mutually-agreed conclusion. If the team is effective, it should make better decisions than any given individual alone. This makes sense because if the team can't do this, why waste resources working together?

From the beginning of the evening one person stood out. He had been with the organisation for a few weeks, and so was the one with the longest service in the room. Throughout the explanation of the vision, mission and policies, his behaviour suggested he was distracted, and a couple of his comments could have been read as sarcastic.

During the exercise, he spoke more than others and directed the actions of the group. Some might identify him as a leader. He carefully laid out his vision and asked the group if they understood and agreed. Hearing no dissent, he carried on and the team finished quickly. When we looked at the results we found that his team had performed worse than any other.

When asked why they thought this was, the group, again, allowed the same "leader" to speak first. He explained that he thought the exercise was "unfair" and that clearly the group didn't have any expertise in survival. Rather than argue with him, I did what any self-respecting coach would do and asked him: "How do you know?"

"What do you mean?" he responded with a note of what I perceived as anger. "Obviously nobody knows anything, or they'd have spoken up! They're grown-ups and they know our results depend on it."

I asked again "But how do you know? Did you actually ask if anyone on the team knew something you didn't? Did you encourage people to speak up?"

He hesitated. Had he? He had asked a couple of questions - he could probably have asked more, but that's just who he is - a "get things done" kind of guy. Apart from that, he hadn't done anything to stop people speaking up and that should be enough.

Unfortunately for him, at that moment, one of the team raised his hand (literally). I said: "You wanted to speak?" and then something amazing happened. It was beautiful. A young Arab guy with pretty poor English opened his mouth and said: "I spent six months working in a desert survival camp."

Time stopped. I looked at him, open-mouthed. Before I could gather my wits the "leader" said "But why didn't you say anything?" It seemed the right question, and we all sat and waited for the survival savant to speak.

"You didn't ask," he said.

My sceptical "leader" was devastated. He prided himself on working well with others and being able to build successful teams, yet he had failed to get others to speak up and tell him information vital to the success of his mission.

He had failed at his self-appointed task of leadership, by not realising just how easy it is to "squash" others - particularly if their filters leave them less likely to take the risk of speaking up in the first place.

WORKHARD 100

We "squash", or go speechless, when we feel unsafe. Neither of these behaviours build trust. In both cases, it's a vicious cycle. People don't give trust, so they don't get it in return, and it goes round and round.

We need psychological safety. This is about being able to trust what your colleagues are saying; being able to trust that you will be listened to on your merits.

You want to feel safe that you won't be shouted down or ignored because of where you sit on the hierarchy, or where you come from, because of your gender, or maybe even because somebody is having a bad day.

As we see in Patrick Lencioni's excellent book, *"Five Behaviours of a Cohesive Team"*[51], without trust, there is no foundation on which to build and get results:

Focusing on... **Results** — Focus on Collective Outcome

Embracing... **Accountability** — Full Attainment of Commitments

Achieving... **Commitment** — Clarification and Buy-In

Mastering... **Conflict** — Constructive Debate

Building... **Trust** — Vulnerability Without Fear of Repercussions

The more diversity there is, the harder it is to build safety. It's not impossible, but as we've seen, there is a need to work harder to find commonalities, to expose filters and to make it the norm to speak up.

Without trust, people don't speak up. You waste time, get worse decisions and don't implement them as well; which results in added stress, increased costs and a negative impact on the bottom line.

Remember this isn't warm and fluffy – data from Google's Project Aristotle clearly shows psychological safety to be the **number one explanation** of high-performing teams.

IT IS POSSIBLE TO BUILD SAFETY BUT IT TAKES TIME AND EFFORT

*So how do you get people to trust you?
It's both very easy and very hard.
You have to trust them, then show them that you do!*

The first thing that engenders trust is transparency and vulnerability. HardTalk allows and supports that, as we're discovering, but there are other things you can do.

For example, a trust exercise.

❶ Be explicit about the need for trust

All trust exercises suck. They are almost by definition going to make you uncomfortable. This probably won't be any different, but it does send a message that you're going to start to talk about trust. You decide how much to take part, you don't need special clothes, and you can't get physically hurt. The following can be done really easily, in pretty much any situation.

In this exercise we're not working on "Common" Trust - the trust you extend to others that they won't steal the computers if left in the office alone, or deliberately corrupt the database. We assume you have this level of trust. It's the type of trust that we extend to each other when driving. We "trust" people know the rules of the road, will stay on the correct side, and stop at red lights.

This exercise is about building *Psychological Safety* - the kind of trust that means you can be vulnerable in front of the other person without repercussions.

This exercise, the Personal Histories Exercise, comes from the aforementioned book by Patrick Lencioni, *"Five Behaviours of a Cohesive Team"*. It's easy to replicate anywhere. It is typically the first small step teams take to start developing psychological trust. It is not a magic bullet.

PATRICK LENCIONI'S PERSONAL HISTORIES EXERCISE

Each member of the group answers the following three questions. There is no follow up. When the group member has answered all three questions the group says thank you and moves on to the next person. When all group members have completed the exercise, a facilitator can debrief asking participants to share something they didn't know before. The three questions are:

1. **Where did you grow up?**
2. **How many siblings do you have and where do you fall in that order?**
3. **Please describe a unique or interesting challenge or experience from your childhood.**

This is about giving team members an opportunity to demonstrate vulnerability in a low-risk way. It helps team members understand one another at a fundamental level, so they can avoid making false attributions about behaviours and intentions.

It can help us give up some of the Potentials and return to the Truths.

Note that trust exercises are not "team building exercises"

Whether it's finding out which animal your team-mates think you resemble; nearly getting trampled by a horse when trying to 'whisper' to it; getting sweaty in front of your boss as you try to hit a ball for the first time in 20 years, or simply making small talk on a bus while on your way to dinner with people you see every day, a lot of 'team building' does anything but what it's supposed to.

Of course, they have a time and a place, and of course bonding is a good thing, but the minute they become mandatory or awkward, they lose any benefit.

In any case, building trust should not be left to the times when you're building a raft or similar.

It's to important.

The real key, of course, to building trust lies outside trust exercises. It is realising that you're always either building or destroying it. Trust can take a lot longer to build than it can to destroy.

Time spent working as a team helps team work

The US National Transportation Safety Board found that 73 per cent of incidents in its database occurred on an aircraft crew's first day of flying together, before people had the chance to learn through experience how best to operate as a team - and 44 per cent of those took place on a crew's very first flight.[52]

Also, a NASA study[53] found that fatigued crews who had a history of working together made about half as many errors as those who didn't have that level of trust.

Even if your job doesn't involve such high stakes, you'll always find trust useful!

❷ Build a common language

Another way of building trust is to have a common language, where everyone understands the same thing inferred by using the same words.

For example, in the Michaela Community School in Brent, London staff members know when they hear "I'm going to be candid", they need to mentally prepare to take feedback well.

When you give people a common language, they are more likely to have HardTalk, so share this book with colleagues (or even better, buy them their own copy or attend the HardTalk programme together!)

❸ Apologise if you get it wrong

If you do forget your long-term, healthy Purpose and behave in a way that isn't suitable, or that causes the other person to misconstrue your Purpose, then you can always apologise.

Research suggests apologising is rarely a bad thing[54]. The majority of studies indicate that apologies do something very useful indeed: they convert a desire for revenge into willingness to forgive and forget, and move on. In business, people are more likely to work with you again if you say sorry. But we sometimes worry that it will make us weak.

Apologising doesn't mean grovelling or debasing yourself. People who demand that of you aren't asking for an apology. They are asking for submission, and that is quite a different thing.

An apology, first and foremost, communicates a simple message that affirms your humanity and that of the injured party: "I see, and I care".

But you've got to get the apology right!

You can get more resources about the perfect apology via *HardTalk.info*

What can you apologise for?

Even if you think you've done nothing wrong, chances are high, if you haven't been a HardTalker in the past, that there's one thing you can absolutely apologise for: the role you've played in allowing the issue to continue longer than it needed to.

To explain this, we often use the metaphor of house-training a puppy.

When you welcome a puppy into your house, you accept that it does not see the world in the same way you do. You understand the puppy is not wrong or deliberately upsetting you - they simply don't understand what you need.

How you react to the puppy's behaviour will be the main lever in that puppy's behaviour. If the puppy pees in the corner and you immediately make it clear that you not happy and there are repercussions, and are explicit in what you want to see instead, you can expect to see some changes in the puppy's behaviour.

If, on the other hand, you say and do nothing then do not be surprised if, in a few months, that puppy is peeing with abandon. That's on you. We accept the standard we walk past. And if we change our mind we need to own that. If the behaviour we've accepted in the past is no longer acceptable, we need to acknowledge our role in having allowed it to continue and speak up now.

CHANGING YOUR BEHAVIOUR IS THE ONLY THING THAT CHANGES YOUR RESULTS

So how did the "emotionally stunted" CFO we mentioned earlier do in building a great team?

At first, he hated it, felt unnatural doing all the things he knew were needed, like meeting people and making connections.

And he really hated the Trust exercise.

During it he told people that he was an only child with distant elderly parents and so grew up solitary. Some of his team shared more, others less. It did make an immediate difference, though, as the team felt closer and more confident they could share things without retribution.

But on return to the "real world" it started to slip, and he occasionally screwed up badly by, for example, shutting down debate with: "Don't be silly, it's obvious what we need to do" or asking with what seemed genuine curiosity: "Are you being stupid on purpose?"

What did make a difference was that, during the Trust exercise and regularly afterwards, he asked for and got feedback or, rather, "feed forward" insofar as he asked what he should do more, or less, of.

He learned to apologise when his behaviour didn't match his Purpose (for example, he said he wanted people to speak but then interrupted.)

Eventually he was a sufficiently different person that clients noticed, and mentioned it. A little after that he plucked up the courage to trust some of these clients enough to talk about it - to admit he wasn't perfect. He was amazed to find it strengthened his client relationships, and is convinced that his new found vulnerability has even lead to new work.

He had been worried originally that he wouldn't be believed. All he did was change his behaviour so it achieved the Purpose he genuinely wanted, and he was transparent about doing so. Whatever you tell people about your Purpose, they'll work it out for themselves based on your behaviour.

If you're thinking it's not my Purpose I need to worry about, it's my boss's (or spouse's or colleague's), don't worry we'll get there.

Right now it's about you!

Are your behaviours always genuinely consistent with what you want? Are you sure you never behave "badly" in the moment? You never sacrifice what you want in the long-term for what feels good in the short-term?

We now move on to the SpeakSoft and Listen Hard sections of the book - what you probably thought you'd be spending most of your time on. But remember, you won't be able to do any of the relatively easy things you need to do to effectively speak and listen, if you don't get your head straight first.

If you don't remember your Purpose in the moment, your behaviour will deteriorate. If you allow Homer to take over you're likely to make decisions that lead to suboptimal results.

The success of any HardTalk really lies inside of you.

CHAPTER SUMMARY

- *"Remind yourself to avoid the Fundamental Attribution Bias – when we think other people's bad behaviour is their fault and ours the result of external circumstances"*

- *"We must remember our true Purpose at all times in order to make sure our behaviour and the way we are perceived match our ultimate goal and will get us the results we want"*

- *"Avoid confusion or offense by: sharing your purpose explicitly, being consistent and using contrasting to make your Purpose clear"*

- *"Teams that have vulnerability-based trust (the belief you can do things or make mistakes without fear of resentment) perform far better than those with just common trust"*

- *"Build psychological safety by: being explicit about the need for trust (using exercises if needed), building a common language to ensure common understanding and apologising if you get it wrong and making apologising part of the culture"*

BE HEARD

CHAPTER 6

*Your organisation **needs** you to speak up. Even if you have a difficult boss, or work in a political environment. Using the 'Declare-Explain' framework, you can talk about pretty much anything.*

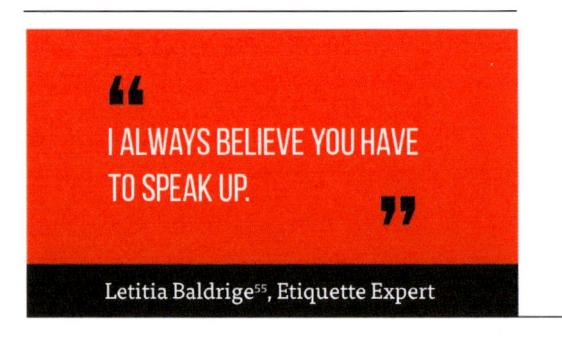

> **I ALWAYS BELIEVE YOU HAVE TO SPEAK UP.**
>
> Letitia Baldrige[55], Etiquette Expert

SPEAKING UP EFFECTIVELY IS YOUR JOB - AND KEY TO YOUR SUCCESS

The joy of our work is helping people to change. The saddest aspect is watching people settle for miserable situations that they could change.

They say humans are the most adaptable of creatures. This is a good thing because it means we can live with almost anything, but it's also bad as then we end up living with things we shouldn't. This adaptability is apparent in our ability to build solutions that allow us to live in places for which we are not physically suited. It's also apparent in our tendency to not notice how bad things have got until it's too late.

In the case of HardTalk, the result is no change and a situation that is more likely to get worse than improve.

We spent a lot of time in Chapter 1 looking at whether you should speak up or not. Here, we're assuming you've decided it's important enough, you can't let it go and you think you've got some hope of making a difference.

Even if it's a small difference. We're also assuming you've done all the hard work to prepare you to speak.

If you work at Michaela Community School in Brent, UK, you are probably used to unusual things, insofar as you are part of a movement

CHAPTER 6 | 1.0
BE HEARD

that is not always well received by the larger teaching community.

You may have seen people demonstrating outside your school, you will have seen the school mentioned regularly (both favourably and otherwise) in the national press, and you may even have received death threats.

In this environment, perhaps being expected to speak up should not be surprising.

Receiving an email like this might be though: "Before the end of the week you must say something to someone that you would not otherwise have said. Start with "In the spirit of candour..."

But this is what teaching staff at the school receive.

The email will then go on to remind the staff member to give both themselves and their HardTalk partner a star on the "Candour Star Chart" in the staff room.

This is because Headteacher Katharine Birbalsingh, one of the most controversial leaders in the UK, understands that: "If you want your organisation to run well, you need to address the fact that the issue of candour, or lack of it, will CRUSH your organisation."

She explains that: "Wherever you work, I guarantee there will be misunderstandings and miscommunication. I guarantee people around you will do things that will make you raise an eyebrow. It is the nature of working with others."

And her solution? Get people to speak up!

"I think staff probably think, 'Oh no... here she goes again...' when they get emails like this from me. But they do as I ask, and they raise all sorts of grievances with their colleagues as a result. What happens next? The grievance gets resolved. No one is left feeling awkward about stuff, wishing they had said something but never quite mustering up the nerve."

Needless to say the Headmistress at Michaela never gets any stars on the chart - because she is always candid.

Hard to take? Perhaps. But people get used to it, and it certainly saves time and energy. Katharine explains further: "Our so-called 'PM (Performance Management) meetings' with me tend to go like this: Me: 'Is there anything we could do to support you better?' Staff: 'Well, no, because had there been, I would have told you.'"

You should only abolish targets in a culture of candour.

When everyone speaks freely to each other, you can get rid of a lot of bureaucracy and target setting. You can get rid of the tick box exercises that pretend to improve people, when in fact they only make an organisation feel as if that's what it is doing.

And the reward for speaking up? At Michaela, the staff get public recognition and chocolate. But your reward is being heard and hearing others, making better decisions and seeing those decisions implemented more effectively and with less stress.

Candour creates a culture of trust. And a culture of trust allows you to abandon a lot of the nonsense that wastes time and energy.

Speaking up effectively is probably part of the expectations your organization has of you. Even if it's not made as explicit as at the Michaela Community School. If you're ambitious, it's fundamental to your success. If you don't speak up, you can never make a difference - and making a difference is what human beings are rewarded for.

Even if you have a difficult boss or work in a political environment.

IF YOU SPEAKSOFT YOU INCREASE THE LIKELIHOOD YOU GET THE RESULTS YOU WANT

There's a few interesting things to note about this second Phase of the HardTalk model: SpeakSoft.

02 SpeakSoft™

SpeakSoft™ - declaring and explaining in a way that minimises defensiveness and shows your best motives

The first thing is that it's the only phase where you are actually talking - being heard.

That's because getting your head straight before speaking is key, and being heard is only half of HardTalk. Hearing is the other half, and we'll look at that in ListenHard.

This is the only place where we talk about the actual words you'll use - because having a difficult conversation effectively is an art. We're trying to give you principles, so you can do HardTalk for yourself rather than a "listicle" of do's and don'ts. A listicle or recipe isn't possible because other people are involved - it's messy! We want to give you the tools to be able to have successful HardTalk, no matter the subject or those involved, every time.

The other interesting thing is that it's the only phase that's "Soft".

But be very clear: that doesn't mean you don't get to say everything that's in your head.

You just have to say it softly by remembering to "Declare and Explain".

We need to hear and be heard.

Being heard means speaking softly, or speaking up in a way that allows people to understand and act on what you say. It's speaking in a way designed to reduce combativeness or defensiveness. This is not a magic bullet, but it does help. So, let's get to it!

DOING THE TWO STEP

Declare and Explain is a two-step model, underlying, once again, the need to "translate" what you want to communicate so the message received, (after it has gone through your HardTalk partner's filters), is the one you want them to get.

This "declaration followed by invitation" model is designed to increase the odds that the other party will be willing to hear your point of view and, along with the skills in ListenHard, to be heard - to share their point of view honestly.

Of course, in a real HardTalk you will use all these skills at the same time, but we teach them separately. When you rehearse your HardTalk you'll see how they all come together.

Rehearsal – with feedback - is a huge part of improving your HardTalk skills. We spend a lot of time on this during the HardTalk training programme, and afterwards through our online and in-person follow up. Without professional help it can be very difficult to get useful feedback.

To help, we've made Feedback Sheets available at ***www.hardtalk.info/resources***

CHAPTER 6 | 10
BE HEARD

THE FATAL FEW SECONDS

The way you begin a difficult discussion or HardTalk can determine its fate. If you immediately trigger defensiveness or combativeness in the other person, the chances of a productive outcome drop to nearly zero.

But if you know how to bring up difficult issues in ways that set the other person at ease, you increase the odds in your favour, no matter what the topic.

We start by "declaring", which may sound dramatic but is, in fact, done respectfully and with humility.

❶ Declare

In the declaration phase you "declare" what you want to discuss. In other words, you succinctly and confidently state your Truths. You provide the basis of all the rest of the HardTalk. But how do you do that? What criteria can we use to judge how well you are speaking softly?

D1 *Ask for permission*

To make sure that you start SpeakSoft right, ask for permission.

"Hi, Dave. Are you available to talk? I think we need to spend some time talking about that last meeting. Do you have time now?"

Why should we ask for permission?

Remember we are in the business of trying to hear and be heard. To do that we need to show respect and not try to "win" the conversation or "beat" the other person. Asking if they want to talk with you is a good start to showing respect.

We also don't want to find ourselves in a situation where we build up our courage, start to speak and then find the other person has no time for us.

Lastly, it acts as a kind of "topic marker". It gives your HardTalk partner a heads up that something is coming, even if you haven't yet been clear about what it is.

The Sandwich

Don't use the Praise Sandwich! You may have heard about the "praise sandwich" before: it's recommended in lots of training courses and is sometimes referred to by a rather less refined but more alliterative phrase*. Despite its ubiquity, however, it's a very bad idea.

Butter them up

Get to the meat of the issue

Sweeten Them Up

It sounds good. As you can see in the image the idea is to "tell them something good", then give them "constructive feedback", and then tell them something good again. It's what's happening when someone says something like: "Hey, do you have a minute? I wanted to say you did a great job at the presentation last week. But I thought the level of detail was wrong - I fell asleep three times. But your tie

---

*"The "sh!t sandwich"

SPEAKSOFT 110

looked great. OK? Byeeee..."

That's maybe a rather extreme example, but I would be prepared, if I gambled, to bet a large amount of money that you recognise it. It's widespread and many of those using it think they're doing the right thing.

The problem is it doesn't work.

Think about what happens in your head when this is done to you. What do you remember feeling? Most likely, you first experienced immediate trepidation upon hearing, "Hey, do you have a minute?", followed by interest at the "I wanted to say you did a great job at the presentation last week".

However, as you waited for the inevitable "but" that experience has taught you to expect, you switched to resignation over the "constructive" *(read: negative and often unactionable)* feedback, "But I thought the level of detail was wrong - I fell asleep three times."

You probably didn't even hear the nice compliment they finished up with because you're thinking about the fact they fell asleep!

It's not a respectful technique because it aims to distract and somehow "sneak up" on the person on the receiving end of the feedback. You can test whether it's respectful in one simple way: Imagine explaining the technique to a mentee.

"I'm going to tell my colleague something nice (but probably unrelated and possibly unimportant) which they're not going to hear anyway because I always follow up with something negative or, as I like to call it, the real reason I'm talking to them and then, so that they leave good and confused I'll finish up with a compliment."

You wouldn't tell someone you were going to do that because it's crazy!

Some people bring up Performance Reviews as a defence of this technique, pointing out that if you didn't include both positive as well as negative feedback, the review would be a miserable experience, not to mention unrealistic and unfair.

My response to that is simple. Performance Reviews should not be HardTalk.

Official performance reviews are a box-ticking exercise you need to do because, sadly, not all leaders or managers can be trusted to do their job of leading and managing others by having these conversations "little and often".

Managing the performance of others is your job if you're a manager or leader, and so should be happening all the time. It's a continuous process. The Performance Review should be a matter of "doing the necessary" for the audit trail, not a litany of bad things you need to bring up and "leaven" with a little positive patting on the head. Nor should you let things drag on until annual reviews.

It comes back to respect. The business world is fast moving and needs people, at all levels, who can be trusted to behave like grown-ups.

One way of building that trust is to actually treat people like grown-ups!

The real test, of course, is does the praise sandwich work? Do people who get feedback in this way tend to use that feedback and make changes that are useful to themselves, their teams and their results? The research suggests not.[56]

If we are given vague, negative feedback, hidden among other more easily-digested feedback, we tend to focus on what makes us feel better.

We're hardwired to avoid cognitive dissonance. This is especially true if we've gone a year since our last performance review

CHAPTER 6 | 10
BE HEARD

with no negative feedback. We think we're doing great, but when we enter our one-to-one Performance Review, we are told that we are doing well in two areas, but not so well in another.

The relative importance of those things and what we are supposed to do about them may not be clear, and so the message risks not getting through.

This isn't to say we don't think people should be praised. On the contrary, we say praise often and praise well.

Be specific and, ideally, praise as the other likes being praised *(please don't ever praise me in public as it makes me blush!)*. But please don't praise during HardTalk.

Instead, praise separately. When you're in a HardTalk scenario: focus on the Hard message.

We ask permission to show respect, we confirm time is available and we open channels of communication. But what if we don't get these things? What if the other person says no?

For example: "Hey Jan, do you have time to talk?" "No, sorry, I'm going into a meeting."

This sometimes happens. If so, then it's easy. You make an appointment for the future. But what if it happens a few times or there are cancellations? In that case it's about going back to the three-step process including Pain/Ache/Emergency (see Chapter 1) and considering having a different HardTalk! For example, about the fact that your HardTalk partner seems to be avoiding you.

D2 *Focus on one topic*

Focus on just one topic in your HardTalk conversation: concentrate on building a shared understanding about the behaviour you're discussing and then work together to decide next steps.

This approach is more useful to both partners, and will result in decisions about future actions that are more likely to be implemented.

Focusing on one topic allows you to connect it to the long-term purposes that you both care about. By identifying barriers and putting in place effective follow up procedures, you can establish how improving this one thing will improve other things.

All of this is an approach you could share with anyone without shame, unlike the Praise Sandwich.

D3 *Start with the Truths*

Start your HardTalk with the Truths: the things you've seen and heard.

Really make sure that these are, in fact, Truths and not your interpretation of the Truths.

Would everybody in the world recognise these Truths? If so, then these are the least controversial things you could say (even if they are hard to say) and, until they're agreed, there's no point going on.

If the person you are talking to is so far away from you that you can't agree on what you see and hear, then you need to be talking about something else or building evidence.

When declaring your Truths, be as concrete and specific as possible. This is essential. Avoid speaking only in vague generalities and don't

SPEAKSOFT 112

mention your Potential yet!

Don't worry about sugarcoating or softening what you're saying - all you're saying are Truths, right?

We've already spoken about the need to take responsibility and apologising. If you have a role of any kind - if you should have had the conversation earlier - if there is anything you should have done differently, consider acknowledging it at this stage. Pretending you didn't do something doesn't mean everyone doesn't know (even if they pretend)!

We also want to acknowledge our emotions. Some of these HardTalk scenarios are very tricky. It's ok to be anxious, and it's ok to tell the other person you are.

It's hard to tell someone they smell, or are being fired, or are making you think they're unreliable. It's ok to admit that.

Just don't make it all about you - that's a sub-category of a "topper" *(someone who must always be better than you in a conversation - see Chapter 7)*.

> *When you know you're going to be giving bad news it's reasonable to be worried. When you're telling somebody you like and know well that they're not going to have a job in a few weeks, it's normal to have some emotions and to share them. This might sound something like: "Barack, do you have some time to talk? I've got some bad news. This isn't easy for me to say, but I want you to know that I like you and want to make this as painless as possible. I'm afraid you've been let go."*
>
> What it **shouldn't** sound like is: "Barack, do you have some time to talk? I've got some bad news. I haven't slept all night thinking about it and I hope you don't hate me - I did try really hard to make your case but I'm afraid you've been let go."
>
> *This, believe it or not, is how a manager of our acquaintance explained he had told one of his direct reports he no longer had a job. He couldn't understand why there was a problem!*

D4 Watch your language

When we talk about "language" we're talking in terms of the actual language you use and "body" or "non-verbal", language. In both cases, you can say the same thing in different ways and your intention can easily be misunderstood. The way you "say" something - whether words, gestures, body language or tone of voice - is a form of communicating.

Don't forget that you're "speaking" even when you're not using words - are you coming across as you want to? Given the filters of the person you're speaking with?

As difficult as it is to get feedback on non-verbal language, it can be equally tricky to get the verbiage right. Particularly, as we'll see, when you're working across cultures and languages.

> Both statements below describe the same situation. They are both equally true, but one is more likely to trigger defensiveness.
>
> *(A) During the executive team meeting yesterday I found out our project is further behind than any other project in our work stream. Unless we catch up, there will be a delay to the project with repercussions for how our team is perceived, and our careers in the short-term at least.*

CHAPTER **6** | 10
BE HEARD

> (B) *I was blindsided in the exec team meeting yesterday when it came out that our team was under-performing. If we don't fix this now it will be career limiting.*
>
> Why? The second comes across as more judgmental and even scolding, which will likely trigger defensiveness. Certain words tend to trigger certain responses.

D5 Avoid judgemental words and extremes

"Always" or "never" are great examples of "extreme" words. As soon as you say something like *"You always forget to pay the dry cleaner!"* or *"You are always late giving me that report"*, you will find yourself in an argument about whether "always" includes the time three weeks ago when the other person actually did pay, or did hand in the report on time.

What is judgmental or extreme depends on the other person's filters.

Some words/phrases that are anathema to you are okay by me. And vice versa. This will be true of everyone.

Other words may be extreme because they cause an "extreme" reaction - a reaction seemingly out of proportion to the word itself. We're not talking about something like a swear word, which should obviously be avoided in the majority of cases. We're talking about words that, for whatever reason connected to their filters, provoke an extreme reaction.

For example, the word "dear" (probably because I'm a woman from Western Europe born in 19??) grates on my nerves. I know this is because of my filters. I know it isn't meant to annoy me, or make me feel disrespected and, mostly, I remember this.

This is important because words have two types of meaning: the *denotative* meaning vs *connotative* meaning.

> The **denotative** meaning is the literal, dictionary description of the word
>
> The **connotative** meaning is what the word suggests to an individual, based on that person's experiences, emotional reactions and judgements associated with the word or what it refers to. In other words, the connotative meaning is what we understand a word to mean, based on our filters

For example - *respect, truth, lie, polite, soon* - these words will have very specific and different meanings to different people - particularly across cultures. That doesn't mean we can't use them, but we need to be aware of how our filters, and those of others, change the meaning.

As we'll see in ListenHard, the trick is to get both yourself and the other person to stick to the Truths.

Exercise:
Your HardTalk scenario - declare your Truths

Look back on page 53 where you wrote your Truths. Underline any language that might be problematic and make a quick note of why. NB: All adjectives are problematic, because they are potentials.

Now start building your HardTalk "script" by rewriting your HardTalk Truths here, avoiding

SPEAKSOFT   114

extreme or judgemental language - and remembering to start by asking for permission.

_____
_____
_____
_____
_____
_____
_____
_____
_____
_____
_____
_____
_____
_____
_____
_____
_____

It comes down to the "Process of Progress." You need to think about the filters. Ask yourself how you're being perceived, or are likely to be perceived, and change your language (actual and body), so it lets you come across as you want.

For example, if you want to come across as interested, don't check your mobile phone.

If you want to come across as respectful that will mean different things to different people, (although the phone thing is pretty universal here too).

We already touched on this earlier when we looked at what perception you want people to have - what Potential you want them to come up with - and you think you know what you need to do - what Truths you need to show them - to get that.

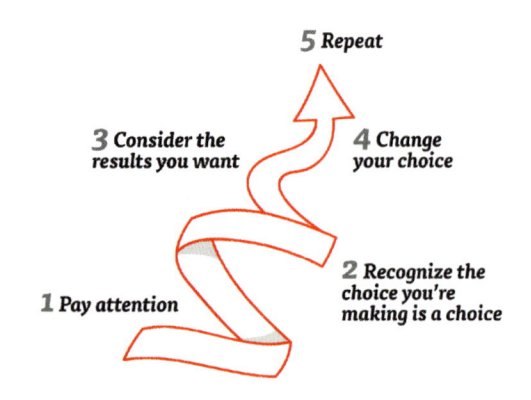

1 Pay attention
2 Recognize the choice you're making is a choice
3 Consider the results you want
4 Change your choice
5 Repeat

D6 Tell some stories

The point of HardTalk is to get the results you want. That is usually about getting people to change their action in some way - to agree to a new strategy, to participate in an event, to follow a process. This means influencing people even (especially?) when you don't have any "power".

Before you can do that, before you can change their actions, you've got to get someone's attention.

Stories, like the many we tell throughout this book, are good for this because we naturally want to know what happens next if it's presented right. Stories allow us to feel empathy, and are a great way to present "lessons" - because we're primed to learn from the experience of others through stories.

It's a sad fact that we live in an age where attention is hard to get and harder to keep.

Just as it's important on a presentation or pitch to get to the point your audience cares about quickly, you need to do the same in HardTalk.

There is a tendency to waffle when we're uncomfortable. I would urge you to use the DecisionTree (available online at hardtalk.

CHAPTER 6 | 10
BE HEARD

info) to help you quickly work through the WorkHard part of HardTalk, hone what you have to say and address the real issues.

By doing this, you can avoid wasting your time and losing the attention of your HardTalk partner.

This brings us to the second part of SpeakSoft.

We've done our declaration - making sure, among other things, that our language and body language was appropriate to our purpose.

Now, in the "Explain" part, we can put context around the Truths, and make sure the other person has every chance to really understand what we're saying, and why we're saying it.

What this boils down to is giving them the chance to really hear us.

2 Explain

In the "Declare" phase of SpeakSoft you've confidently declared your Truths.

But remember your Potentials are how you see the Truths through your filters.

It's possible, in fact probable, that the other person sees the same truths in a different way. Here, you're going to create some awareness, share your context and explain why you "declared" as you did.

E1 Share your Potential

Sharing your Potential means explaining why you bothered Declaring your Truths.

Remember your Potential is just one of many, so you're going to do this carefully and humbly because you are aware you might be wrong.

You might need to change your mind or apologise if you learn something you didn't know.

But, no matter what, remember you're accepting that your Potential might be wrong.

Sometimes you will know for sure that the other person is unaware of one of the Potentials for the Truths.

For example, we had a visitor to Dubai and we went to smoke shisha. He sat with his legs crossed, and the sole of his shoe pointed at some people. We knew he didn't understand the issue with sitting like that, so we explained this new Potential. As you can imagine, he quickly changed position to avoid causing possible *offence*.* Sometimes HardTalk is relatively easy but it's usually more complicated than this.

Often, for example, HardTalk is about holding people accountable. That means making the gap between expectations and action clear - between your perception of the Truths you see, and what you want to experience.

Having conversations about this kind of gap is leadership, at any level of the organisation.

It's not something bosses do - it's something leaders do - with their direct reports (if they have any), their peers and people above them in the hierarchy.

> *Holding people accountable is a good thing - it's how things get done, improved, how the world moves on.*

People need it and want it, and they want to see others being held accountable!

Accountability isn't abuse. It isn't squashing people down and shouting at them, whatever the movies tell us. But they do sometimes need

---

*In Arab culture, and many others, the sole of the shoe or foot is considered dirty, and therefore insulting to show to others.

to know what's likely to happen if their current action doesn't change and we do that here by sharing the consequences.

E2 Share the consequences

Sometimes, particularly when you don't have any positional power, it helps to think of Consequences as being *Natural* and *Official*.

Natural Consequences are the things that happen naturally if we do something. You're not threatening anything - just highlighting the possibilities, probabilities or sure things!

For example, if I jump into a pool I will get wet; if I make my boss look like an idiot in a meeting, I may not have her support at the next promotion panel.

> *A relatively experienced and well-respected junior executive at a regional marketing consultancy was tasked with one deliverable as part of a much larger project. It was her job to make sure that 5,000 brochures were ready for an enormous industry trade fair. Unfortunately, she didn't accurately proofread the document allowing a very rude typo to slip through and so, on the day, the brochures were unusable.*
>
> **The natural consequences of this were that:**
>
> - *she had wasted her time*
> - *she looked "bad" - lazy and / or incompetent in front of her boss and colleagues*
> - *the client received an enormous discount, impacting the bottom line*
> - *somebody else had to have a difficult conversation with the client*
> - *the client didn't have brochures available with implications for sales*
> - *the client considered moving its business elsewhere*

Official consequences are things that you (or your organisation or other authority) can make happen.

If I speed and use my mobile phone I might die, or kill someone - that's a natural consequence. An official consequence is that I might get a speeding ticket, a fine or lose my licence.

When looking at the case of the marketing executive, the official consequences might have included an official warning or disciplinary procedures and performance improvement plans.

Sometimes, of course, you don't have any power or there won't be any official consequences. Let's say you have a boss who puts you down in meetings. You've had a HardTalk and the guy simply tells you "to grow a thicker skin". What can you do?

You have, as always, two options *(see Introduction)* - you can do something or do nothing.

You might decide to leave or make a complaint. You could take responsibility and have another HardTalk about the fact that you're afraid that if he continues to put you down it will...well, what are the Natural Consequences?

Write your thoughts here:

_____
_____
_____
_____

CHAPTER 6 | 10
BE HEARD

Our tendency is to go to official power first, or at least very quickly. Because of the Fundamental Attribution Bias *(see page 88)* we assume behaviour we see is a result of personality.

We either don't try to change it, or choose the wrong levers *(remember: because we see the world through different filters, different things motivate us)* and then we give up and go to official power.

Instead, we should spend more time listening, so we can find more powerful ways to influence others.

We hear more about this later in Chapter 7 when we look at the six things that can enable or hinder people from changing.

Defining and Explaining

Rahul, an associate at one of the big consultancy firms, was upset with his boss who, despite saying all the right things in private about wanting to support, protect and develop her team, consistently made undermining comments about Rahul in public. Rahul clearly had no positional power but (carefully!) used his HardTalk skills to make sure the boss was aware of the natural consequences (a diminished reputation among ambitious employees and so difficulties recruiting and retaining the best people, for example).

Rahul said: "Hi Lina, do you have a couple of minutes to talk about something? I'm loathe to bring this up as I know the messenger can easily get shot, and I don't want to upset you in any way. I'm a big fan of yours, and I want to make sure that you're as successful as I know you can be. I also want to pay back the many good things you've done for me.

It's important the consequence be something the person cares about. It is usually best to start with consequences for them, and then work outwards to show potential natural consequences for the people or institutions they care about.

It may take more than one consequence and you're more likely to be able to find the right one if you know the person well. For instance, the consequences, if your boss keeps shutting you down, could be that she might look like a bully; that her behaviour doesn't match company "values"; that other people might not speak up, or that you might not speak up, for example.

If you reach *'Official Consequences'* it should only be once you have exhausted all other kinds of power at your disposal, and are only left with relying on "coercive" or official power.

This doesn't mean you shouldn't use official consequences of course - sometimes you have no choice. Just make sure you follow procedure and, secure in the knowledge you've tried everything else, be confident in your decision.

SPEAKSOFT

I noticed that when I suggested getting an outside supplier you rolled your eyes. You did the same thing on a few other occasions: when I observed we'd failed to make our numbers and last week, at a client meeting, you interrupted me and sighed when I said we'd seen a similar problem in the past.

When you do that, it makes me feel like you want me to stop talking, and I'm concerned that I'm not alone. I know it's important to you that the people you lead develop and grow and move on to better things. I'm afraid the way you treat us sometimes undermines us in front of others, with negative consequences. Negative consequences not only for us, but for you too, because we reflect you. I hope you understand why I'm saying this, and understand that you have my loyalty in any case."

The more we understand who we're working with, the more focused we can be in how we communicate. To use the example of a medical professional, this is just like gaining understanding of a patient's personal circumstances and, eventually, their genome to help personalise the treatment prescribed.

Remember your ultimate purpose in having HardTalk is to hear and be heard. It's to share what you've noticed, the Truths, and put forward a Potential and maybe some Consequences. It's to understand why something is the way it is, and work with the other person to make it better.

If we go straight to official power, if we assume fear is the only thing that motivates, then we assume we need to shout at, or squash, people. No wonder we go speechless either when we should start a HardTalk or, often, if someone starts one with us.

Candour doesn't come easily to anyone, but it is possible with practice and with support.

Whether it's a high-performing school or a market leader llike Facebook, they see candour as the cure for mediocrity. In other words, you can survive by staying quiet, but you won't get better, and nor will anything or anyone else.

CHAPTER SUMMARY

- *"The best performing companies know that a culture of candour is fundamental to good communication and improved performance"*

- *"Ensure you communicate the right message by using the Declare/Explain method"*

- *"Declare: Ask for permission, focus on one topic, start with the truths, watch your language, tell stories and avoid judgemental extremes"*

- *"Explain by sharing your Potential and sharing the consequences – but remember to put the Natural ones before the Official ones"*

LISTEN

CHAPTER 7

Listening is fundamental to good communication. Being misunderstood is toxic to performance and HardTalk. When you Invite and Reflect you can build trust with the other person and get the results you want.

> " I ALWAYS BELIEVE YOU HAVE TO SPEAK UP "
>
> Bryant McGill[57], Author

WHEN WE'RE LISTENING, WE'RE MOSTLY NOT

Most of us want to get our point across. We know we've spent a lot of time thinking about the issues and we know our hearts are pure. We want the other person to understand why we're right, and why they're wrong. We probably have great reasons to explain our certainty and are bewildered that others don't simply understand.

What is wrong with these people that they can't understand why what I'm suggesting is good for them? We blame others when they don't understand - they must be stupid or blinded by their emotions, unlike us rational people!

Of course, people aren't generally more stupid than us and they certainly don't experience more emotions - we all experience emotions. They may, indeed, be less adept at controlling their emotions. In that case, we need to help them, as we'll see later, so they can hear us.

In fact, when other people aren't convinced by us we blame them, when we should be blaming ourselves for not listening well enough to be able to effectively influence the people we need to.

Most of us only listen "competitively" - we listen just enough to keep the other person involved. Our intent is to reply and not to understand.

We spend our time preparing what we're going to say next, what questions we're going to ask. We forget we hear everything through filters. We "judge" what we're hearing rather than understanding. Our purpose slips from hearing to replying. We listen to connect to ourselves rather than others - only really getting interested when we have something to "contribute". Real listeners don't do that.

They understand listening is contributing: it's a full contact sport, and isn't something you do when doing something else. Listening is an activity in itself.

WHAT KIND OF RESPONDENT ARE YOU?

It's been suggested that there are four kinds of respondents. Do you recognise yourself here? Other people?

❶ Evaluators

Evaluators will consider any statement they're faced with, no matter how innocuous, assess it and then either agree or disagree. For example, if the conversational gambit were: "I just went to what I think is one of the best surfing beaches in the world last week - Arugam Bay in Sri Lanka" an Evaluator might respond with: "I think the beach in Manapad Point is better - especially if you're a novice."

❷ Probers

When faced with the same statement, a Prober will ask questions but from their own frame of reference. So, in this case, the Prober might say something like: "Oh, is it good for beginners? I just started learning to surf a couple of weeks ago!"

Probers are interested, and will point to the questions they ask as proof of this. The breadth of their interest far outstrips the depth though.

❸ Advisors

Like the Evaluators and Probers, Advisors act from a good place. They want to give counsel, to advise, and to create solutions to problems. In short, they want to help.

In the case above they might respond with: "Oh, I know a much cheaper place just 10 kilometres away," and this might, indeed, be helpful, or it might be entirely inappropriate.

They often try to help too soon - without spending time finding out everything they can. This has a number of consequences. It's short-sighted because, as we saw earlier, everyone sees the world differently. Despite this, we tend to think people will just change their minds if we explain things to them. Instead, we need to see beyond our filters, and help them see beyond theirs, to the Truths. Then you can communicate. You can give advice that is *actually* helpful.

❹ *Interpreters*

Interpreters are a little like Probers and Evaluators in that they analyse others' motives and behaviours based on their own experiences.

All of these responses are equally (un) reasonable at different times. But it's not about the perfect response – which is impossible to predict without knowing everything about a situation. It's about being aware of what results you want, and the results you're getting; noticing when there's a gap and changing your behaviour to bridge that gap.

Does culture matter when trying to ListenHard?

People often ask if HardTalk is harder for some people than for others. By that they almost always mean: "I think my/their culture/age/ background makes it harder to speak up/ ListenHard." In some cases, I've even been told it's not possible for an older man to listen to a younger one without losing face. I call nonsense. On both counts.

Every piece of research suggests while there are some filters in every human being that make elements of HardTalk harder, it's equally true that the same human being will have filters that make other elements easier. You don't get to use your "special circumstances" as a reason not to speak or listen. You can do whatever you want (remember the *Rules of Adulting in the Introduction*), but it's a decision.

What most people have, no matter their filters, is a dislike of confrontation, because when they hear the word they think of strife and unhappiness and bad feeling. When these people understand how little HardTalk is about speaking and actually how respectful it is, because of the focus on hearing and being heard, and not on a prescriptive "listicle", they understand it works across all cultures.

Success in HardTalk is not about culture. It's about putting in the work. Listening is hard, and we see the same problems across all cultures. For example, the following phenomenon seems, according to what we've seen, to be spread evenly across all nationalities.

Toppers and Plussers are alive everywhere

"Plussers" cause others to feel that what they're saying matters in conversations: they build on, or add to, what the other person is saying.

"Toppers" either hijack the conversation abruptly to make it about them, or try to top what the other person is saying, as in: "Ah, that sounds like a nice trip you took to Florida. We went to Fiji." Toppers make people think they weren't listening, but rather waiting for their turn to speak.

For an example, in response to an opening gambit like:

"I thought we could consider outsourcing from South Africa," a "Plusser" might say: "Wow, that's a great idea! Really smart and creative. We could even go one step further and try X, if you think that would work."

A "Topper" would say: "Your idea is good, but I actually ran my idea by our CEO already and he loved it - so maybe we should go with mine."

CHAPTER 7 | 10
LISTEN

Listening is key to HardTalk

Although it's called HardTalk, talking or speaking makes up a very small part of the work. Listening, however, is fundamental to any attempt to communicate effectively.

Without the two parts of listening - inviting and reflecting - we can't check our understanding and confirm that our point is being understood.

Listening means the other person feels heard, which builds trust and gets them to speak up further so that, over time, you ensure better decisions, more effectively implemented.

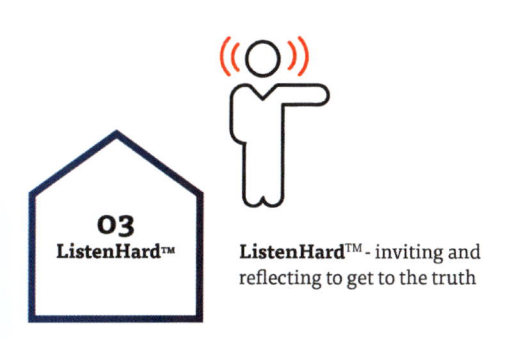

03 ListenHard™

ListenHard™ - inviting and reflecting to get to the truth

When listening it's clearly about Hearing - we're trying to get to and understand their Truths, so we can see through their filters – which tells us how they see the world.

But don't worry. It's also about being Heard because by ListeningHard we can craft our message in a way that makes sense to the other person. As a negotiator (and we're always negotiating!) you will often be dealing with someone who sees the world very differently from you. If you want to get a good result, you'll spend time exploring their world and understanding what makes them tick.

By listening hard, we can learn whether motivation or ability (see Six Sources on page 130) is the problem and whether it's personal, social or structural. We can also identify which consequences are mostly likely to be effective, if and when we do share them.

In other words, Listening Hard is the backbone of the HardTalk model. And, as always, the behaviours themselves aren't difficult. What's difficult is monitoring your behaviour - self-awareness; and being able to change it - self-possession.

> *A very successful senior professional had just made partner, but his colleagues weren't completely thrilled. They loved his client relationships, his knowledge and experience and, to be frank, the business he brought in.*
>
> *But he was a partner now and some of his job was to contribute to the running of the firm - ensuring its continuation over time – but he didn't seem to care about this at all. He spent no time building relationships or bridges and didn't seem to be capable of change.*
>
> *We worked with him and as soon as he realised that he needed to build the same connections internally as he had externally for his own sake, as well as that of the firm and his clients, he was able to do it. He had the skills but just didn't care about using them. The things he needed to do haven't got easier or harder to do - he's just seen the impact on his "bottom line". Now that it's important to him, he's doing them.*

There is a tendency to think listening skills are "soft" so I'm hoping this graphic from the FBI will change your mind.

LISTENHARD 124

Behavioural change stairway model

Active listening → Empathy → Rapport → Influence → Behaviour change

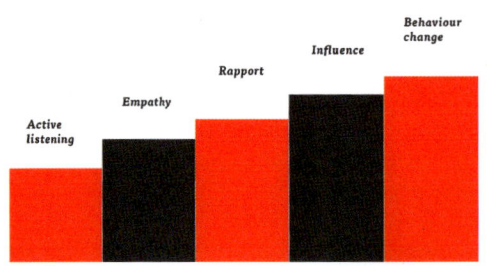

This is what the FBI call the Behavioural Change Stairway Model. Developed by the FBI's Crisis Negotiation Unit, it comprises five stages along which negotiators must guide their partner, (for example, a hostage taker), if they want to get to behavioural change (like giving up the hostage).

The five stages are active listening, empathy, rapport, influence, and, ultimately, behavioural change.

Progression through these stages occurs sequentially and cumulatively. In other words, the negotiator starts at Stage 1 and has to achieve this in order to move to Stage 2 and has to keep up 1 and 2 in order to get to Stage 3. As this process continues, influence (Stage 4) and behavioural change (Stage 5) follow.

You can only get to the successful outcome if and when the previous stages have been carried out successfully.

Look at the Chinese character for listening:

On the top left you have the Chinese "image" for an "ear". This means that you start with your ear. But that's not enough.

On the bottom left we have a character that can mean kingdom i.e. You're listening like the other person is a king.

On the top right there are the elements that mean "10" and "eye" so looking with ten eyes.

And the bottom right a heart symbol.

So, according to the Chinese, what are you giving when you're really listening? Yes, you're lending your ears but you're also giving your full presence, your eyes, your undivided attention and your heart. It's a simple but powerful combination, and it's possible to learn how to do it.

You need to be curious, and humble, and allow for the possibility that what you think is true, is not the case.

This is not about believing everything you are told, but keeping an open mind, and asking more questions than you would normally.

Listen for three things to get better at ListeningHard

ListeningHard - getting other people to speak up - plays a huge part in success and in leading people. It makes a difference to decisions, and implementation of those decisions, as well as to learning and changing. Studies also agree that it's not natural and takes work. However, it is possible.

So why are we so bad at listening? Why won't we let others speak? Why don't we work harder to get them to speak up?

We asked 100 people and got the following nine responses. Do they ring true to you?

> *It's not my job*
> *People should know how to speak up*
> *I don't care about what they have to say*
> *I already know what they're going to say*
> *I don't trust what they're going to say*
> *I am scared of what they might say*
> *I am anxious about the impression I will make in front of others*
> *I get distracted*
> *I don't know what I'm listening for*

Most of these are not things that can be fixed by training, they are more about attitude. Assuming you want to affect behavioural change, we suggest listening for the following three things to help you focus:

1) Facts

2) Emotions

3) Opportunities for questions

If you focus on these three things it will bring you a long way towards becoming an active listener.

We know from the FBI (as well as countless other studies and our own experience) that active listening, when used properly and effectively, displays professionalism, develops rapport and builds trust.

This transcends the world of mediators and hostage negotiators. It is incredibly useful in our interconnected world where, most of the time, we need to get people to do things in situations where just telling them either isn't possible or desirable.

We're now going to look at some skills that are amongst a number of listening techniques taught by the Federal Bureau of Investigation's Crisis Negotiation Unit (FBI CNU) to its special agents and other law enforcement officials from around the world. And they work. But I warn you - you'll know most of them already. Knowing them isn't the problem - implementing them is.

To make them easy to remember, we've split the six different techniques into two categories which reflect what we're trying to do in ListenHard - Invite and Reflect. Firstly, we're going to look at Inviting.

INVITING

Inviting is a big deal - we send pretty cards when we do it. So, make a big deal of it. Think about the right place and time, and the right person. Think about what you are inviting them to do - you're inviting them to trust you. When people are encouraged to talk, they tell us their needs, their wants, their dreams, and their plan of action; in short, they give us information. Which is what we want, but it also gives us power. We must be careful.

The key is to remember your Purpose here. Remember your primary aim is to hear and to be heard.

That focus on hearing and being heard - on understanding so you can influence - is important, but none of us will ever be a perfect listener. Distractions, our filters or our biases will often cause us to miss some important information, or misunderstand a key section of the message. These skills help us to minimise that.

11 Be genuinely curious

If you are really curious, if you really believe you don't know everything about everything and everyone, then this comes across.

UNLESS YOUR NAME IS

Google

STOP ACTING LIKE YOU KNOW EVERYTHING

People can see your curiosity in your body language and in your tone of voice. It's revealed in the type of question you ask (open and follow up), the encouragement you give, the lack of interruption you allow, and the level of distraction you seem to give off, for example.

It's lovely when someone is genuinely curious in you - it feels good. Martin Seligman identifies it as a key character strength that can enhance life satisfaction.[58] If you remember to be curious, things like your tone and body language simply fall into place. But you still need to ask good questions.

What's a good question?

In essence a good question is one where you're really interested in the answer. They tend to be one of the *"Who, What, Where, Why, Why, How"* questions.

But what makes for bad questions? You know, those questions that aren't really questions? What do they sound like? They tend to sound like instructions or comments masquerading as questions.

Examples of good and bad questions:

Good: *What happened? What were you trying to achieve? What would you do differently? Why do you think that?*

Bad: *Why did you let it happen? What were you thinking? Don't you think you could have done x instead? Why don't you do as I told you?*

Any time your intent is wrong, you won't be asking good questions. An example of this is when you're not really asking because you want to understand better you're asking; because you want to make a suggestion, or have the other person guess what's on your mind.

Prepare questions with care if you want good ones. If you find it hard to think of great questions, use other people's – you can download a list of questions from www.HardTalk.info

You can still suggest solutions

Sometimes we work with individuals who know the answer. That's their thing. They can see the point of asking questions and learning more about the person they're hoping to influence, but they baulk at the idea that suggesting a course of action is always wrong. We agree with them.

Sometimes you have to yell: "Fire. Get out!" rather than convene a drum circle to decide on what the group should do.

The focus on listening and questioning doesn't mean you can't give solutions. You can, as long as you are clear that's what you're doing. Don't kid yourself you're just curious when that's not what's going on.

Mostly, a suggestion means you're telling someone what you want them to do. Which is fine, but be clear on that. Don't hide behind suggestions. You can use suggestions when it's really a suggestion. When you're convinced there's no more information you could get and nothing else you could usefully ask then why not offer your opinion. Just don't do it too soon.

Suggestions are also a reasonable tool to use when you've tried everything else. If you've Invited and Reflected, (remember that although these are two sets of skills, you're using them concurrently in any HardTalk scenario), trying to understand what is happening and haven't got anywhere, you might decide to guess.

For example, if your HardTalk partner is reluctant to speak up and tell you what they really think despite your best efforts, you might venture a guess or suggestion as to what you think is really going on.

You might also use suggestions when you want to mention the unmentionable.

If there's an issue that you suspect is on the other party's mind, and you believe he/she is reluctant to bring it up - for whatever reason - you can suggest it. It might sound like this: "I'm still not really clear on why you were so upset in the budget meeting. Did I do something that made you think I wasn't on your side?"

Note that although this is grammatically a question, it is, in fact, a veiled suggestion.

It's fine to use suggestions in this way if your Listening skills aren't getting you the results you want. Remember, this is not about saying you agree with the suggestion. Instead it's about letting the other person know it's okay to talk about it. It means that if they see it that way, you want to hear their point of view and discuss it. You might end up seeing it their way or you might not.

Suggestions can be especially useful in situations where you are trying to get someone who has less power than you to open up. It shows that you've thought about the issue, which shows you care about the person.

The downside of mentioning the unmentionables is, of course, that you might "put ideas in their head" or make the other party think that your mentioning it means you condone it. If that's not the case, you will need to be clear about that.

12 Stay quiet

The second skill in Inviting is using silence effectively.

The first and most important reason to stay

quiet is that you can't listen if you're talking. It's a coincidence of course - but a happy one - that 'Listen' is made up of the same letters as 'Silent'!

LISTEN
SILENT

Most of us are uncomfortable with silence, despite its power to help us learn, but when you're quiet you can't mess up and say something you shouldn't.

Try this:

In a large group of people ask everyone to be quiet. Listen carefully for 30 seconds. See what happens. How do people react? Mostly they'll seem nervous and many groups won't get to the end without somebody blurting out a comment or giggling.

A major difference between expert negotiators and non-experts is that experts listen much more than they speak.

This isn't surprising: when we listen well, we gain the trust and confidence of others.

You can't make a mistake when you're not speaking.

You might even learn something!

Many of us tend to fill in the (silent) gaps, when we could use them to control the negotiation process by simply listening well. Most of us find silence difficult, and will try to fill it. We can learn valuable information, and perhaps enhance our agreement, by using this "'pregnant pause".

Don't forget, some people process more slowly. It might take them a little longer to get there, or be nervous about speaking up, but they may have valuable insights to add. Silence gives them more space to be heard.

Silence, in other words, can be used to both soothe and probe.

13 Signal encouragement

By signalling encouragement, our third way of "Inviting", we telegraph that we are listening and encourage the other person to continue. We can do this verbally through simple things like such as "mmm," "okay," and "I see," and of course there are nonverbal or physical gestures, like head nodding. These signals further establish the building of rapport with the person, by us subtly inviting them to continue speaking.

Again, this behaviour simply means that we provide a sign of recognition to the speaker, we are not agreeing with the content of their speech.

So, we've looked at three parts to Invite in ListenHard -

- Show genuine curiosity and ask good questions
- Use silence to smooth and to probe
- Signal encouragement

Listening is hard. To make it easier ask about, and listen for, **the Six Sources of influence**[59]:

	Motivation	Ability
Personal	Do they want to engage In the behavior? **Make the undesirable, desirable**	Do they have the right skills and strengths to do the right thing? **Help them surpass their limits**
Social	Are other people encouraging and/or discouraging behaviors **Harness peer pressure**	Do others provide the help, information and resources required at particular times? **Find strength in numbers**
Structural	Are systems rewarding the right behaviours and discouraging ineffective ones? **Design rewards and demand accountability**	Is the physical and metaphorical environment making it easy to do the right thing? **Change the environment**

Even with the framework above, it can be difficult to remember to keep listening, as the human tendency is to want to jump in.

One way we see this is in our readiness to assume the reason for someone's behaviour lies primarily in their motivation. We believe if someone is correctly motivated they will, magically, turn into a star performer. Clearly a moment's thought makes it obvious this is untrue. For example, you could offer me a million dollars to learn how to create pivot tables in Excel before close of business and, despite feeling motivated, I would be unable to achieve that objective - I simply don't have the ability.

These two "explainers" - motivation and ability - are always the reason for somebody not behaving as we'd like. But it's not just personal motivation and ability: one's peers come into play too.

In the second row of the Six Sources we can see the behaviour of the people around you makes a difference to your ability and motivation to behave in a given way.

For example, your peers may not value certain behaviour (e.g. leaving on time) and so you may find yourself pressured to behave in a way they do value. Or it might be that you depend on your peers for resources to behave in a certain way. If those resources aren't available, even if all the other five sources of influence are aligned, you will not behave as expected.

The third row looks at "things" rather than people. Under structural motivation we would expect to see salaries, bonuses and other forms of compensation.

On the ability side are things like the physical structure. For example, at Google they make it more likely that people will work across silos by ensuring free food is always available - because we are all like, and gather around, free food.[60]

REFLECTING

The second part of the ListenHard phase is to reflect - you've stayed quiet, you've asked questions well, you've signalled encouragement. Now it's time to reflect.

Even if you're good at Inviting, you have to improve your Reflecting skills to really be able to ListenHard. Few of us do this as much as we should - mostly because we feel stupid or (and this is much worse) aren't interested!

So let's think about it. What can you Reflect?

You can only Reflect what is there i.e. the

Truths and the Potentials you've created about those Truths.

So, you can Reflect back

the Truths (what you see and hear)

your Potentials (what you think about what you hear and see)

their Potentials as you see them i.e. what you think is going on with them

If you Reflect only the Truths, then that's a start. But it may confuse people who don't see the world in the same way we do. For example, I might say to someone: "You've turned up 50 minutes after the time we agreed, and have not brought any business cards."

This Reflects the Truths. If the person sees the world in the same way I do, they will understand that I am implying they are unprofessional and feel the need to provide an excuse that I would feel would justify their lateness. However, most people don't see the world as I do, so I need to Reflect the Potentials as well.

This is where we build rapport and relationships quickly because we're sharing our interpretation of what is going on. If what is going on is negative, then building awareness of that by Reflecting it can begin the conversation. It helps us and our partner to make decisions with all of the information in place.

For example, I might continue the conversation by explaining my interpretation: "This makes me think you aren't as concerned as I am about being seen as professional. Can you help me understand what's going on?"

As we saw earlier, the tone of voice and body language you use will be critical here.

We should Reflect for lots of reasons

We Reflect to confirm our understanding of what's going on, and understand the other party's point of view. We need to do this if we're to learn, and either change a mind or make a credible decision.

There is one caveat in all this listening of course. Watch out! You might have to change your mind. We reflect to show that we've heard and understood. This might mean reflecting on a newly-posed Potential or new information, and changing your mind. You must do this if you're ListeningHard.

The first technique in Reflecting is well known, but not used as much as it should be - it's paraphrasing.

R1 *Paraphrase*

A paraphrase

- *Repeats what the person said in your own words*
- *Includes the elements important to the person as well as acknowledging the person's emotions*
- *Is a CLOSED question - in other words it can be answered with a "Yes" or "No" answer*
- *Starts with a prefix - e.g. "So what you're saying is.?", "Are you saying", "So you seem to be saying", "So you think that...?", "It sounds like...? etc.*

When you look at the definition of paraphrasing it's immediately apparent why it's the number one reflecting tool. Paraphrasing is one of the most useful things

CHAPTER 7 | 10
LISTEN

you can do - particularly across cultures - and is horribly underused.

> I was once teaching paraphrasing to a group of mentors when one of them said excitedly: "Oh, I know about this. It's great! I learned about it on another course and when I said something sceptical about it the facilitator paraphrased what I said. This took the wind out of my sails, so I decided to try it myself."
>
> In front of the class I said: "So you weren't convinced until you saw the power of paraphrasing in action for yourself?" To which the mentor said: "Exactly!", looking pleased to be understood so well.
>
> There was a half-beat until she realised paraphrasing had worked again!

Paraphrasing:

- Confirms understanding and so allows you to fix mistakes
- Builds rapport as your partner feels understood
- Helps you to go back to System 2 thinking
- Helps develop trust

Notice how useful these things are in negotiation, decision making, collaboration - all things we care about, and in which to be successful you need to be able to do the above. Whenever you need to influence the other party to reappraise their situation and consider alternatives, paraphrasing can help.

Exercise:
Paraphrasing

1. I'm not sure these results are what the Senior Leadership Team is expecting

"So you feel the SLT will be disappointed?"

2. I don't think the person you are dealing with in the client organization is senior enough to move this project forward

"So you feel I'm never going to get this project up and running?"

3. I don't believe you should be spending so much of your time working on this client

"So you're saying I'm wasting my time?"

4. I'm not convinced of the potential to scale this project

5. I'd like to take your suggestion to the Senior Leadership Team for their feedback

6. The last three interns we had found some difficulties adjusting to the culture in that team

7. My partners and I are currently in the middle of raising funding for a new business we are launching

LISTENHARD   132

8. When he presented the numbers the client rolled his eyes and snorted

_____
_____
_____

9. I thought I would scream when she asked me about the report for the third time this week

_____
_____
_____

10. This approach has failed every time we've tried it before

_____
_____
_____

11. I feel your priorities have changed since I came on board and you're now more focused on other regions

_____
_____
_____

12. If I knew what I was doing then I'd be happy to help

_____
_____
_____

R2 Mirror

Our second reflecting technique is mirroring. Mirroring has two meanings:

a) You mirror the other person.

This means subtly mirroring their body language, tone of voice or gestures. This helps in many ways. It keeps you focused on what's going on with the other person and it helps build rapport with them, because by mimicking their expression you're gaining some insight into it. Mirroring can be very effective, but it can also be a disaster when overdone.

b) You show the other person a mirror.

Metaphorically! Mirroring can also mean holding up a mirror i.e. showing your Hardtalk partner what they look like to you. For example, if they roll their eyes when you talk to them, you might want to tell them that (the Truth) and tell them what it means to you (the Potential).

For example: "I noticed that when I suggested ABC you rolled your eyes. You did the same thing on a few other occasions, like when I observed XYZ. When you do that it makes me feel like you want me to stop talking. Is that correct or am I missing something?"

Or perhaps: "I've asked you three times to give me a status update and each time you've stammered, gone red and found a reason to leave quickly. I'm starting to think that there's a problem you're not telling me about. Is that correct, or am I missing something?"

Obviously, the potential you choose will depend on your filters and you need to make sure the language is appropriate, i.e. to SpeakSoft.

Many years ago, when I first started my own company, I was invited to meet the regional CEO of a very prestigious multinational organisation. He asked me to tell him what I did. I enthusiastically launched into my

> "pitch", only for him to fold his arms, frown slightly, squint at me and sit back in his chair.
>
> He clearly wasn't interested. Interested people don't look like that. So, I tried something else. He shifted slightly and maybe raised an eyebrow but other than that there was no discernible change. I spent an hour with a man who seemed to hate everything I had to say, and then went home. I cried for an hour, then submitted a proposal, sure that it was pointless but not knowing what else to do.
>
> A few weeks later I signed a contract for a piece of work that took in three layers of management across the whole EMEA region. It was marvellous. It turned out that the man I spoke to looked like that when he was happy. He was famous for it. Nobody had told me however. I hadn't thought of the need to calibrate, so endured the negative feelings, rather than mirroring and questioning my own potential.

R3 Label

We looked at this earlier from a different point of view, when we looked at labelling our own emotions to get Homer, aka System 2, under control.

Here, we're using it to reflect the actions and emotions of the other person. But it's the same idea. Labelling your emotions can have an impact on your ability to manage them. When we label emotions for other people, it can help them to descend the Ladder to Action to their Truths, and so gain control.

Again, you must do this carefully. With other people there are lots of hints - adjectives, adverbs, facial expressions, tones of voice - but the risk is getting it wrong. You need to calibrate! This is particularly true when working across cultures, where the clues or Truths are more likely to be misinterpreted.

The better you are at labelling, (the more specific you are at naming emotions), the more your brain can manage the tasks needed. Researchers think this might be because the more precise your granularity, the more likely you are to do something.

For example, if you are forced to do something you feel is unethical you might "feel bad" but if you think of it as "righteous indignation" you are more likely to do something.

So be as specific as you can in your labelling.

You can also use labelling to get the other person to reflect too, simply by asking them to react to your labelling. For example, "you seem angry?". This is helpful as it moves them to System 2. It allows them to re-engage the executive part of the brain, and make better decisions based on their long term purpose. This is based on the Conceptual Act theory.

> The Conceptual Act theory makes a distinction between the on-going momentary categorisations that create phenomenal consciousness (the content of what you experience), and the self-categorisations that occur when people engage in reflective consciousness (your ability to explicitly label and report on what you experience).

One word of caution, when you label for others, it's a Potential: your understanding of what you see and hear your partner doing and saying. So SpeakSoft when Labelling.

That means starting with your Truth, and then sharing your Potential. It also means being okay with the Potential being wrong, because you're humble enough to admit you don't know everything about everyone. It's ok if your interpretation of the Truths was wrong!

Even if you were wrong in your interpretation, you still helped the other person work out what they were feeling. This helped them get back in control which is, presumably, what you want.

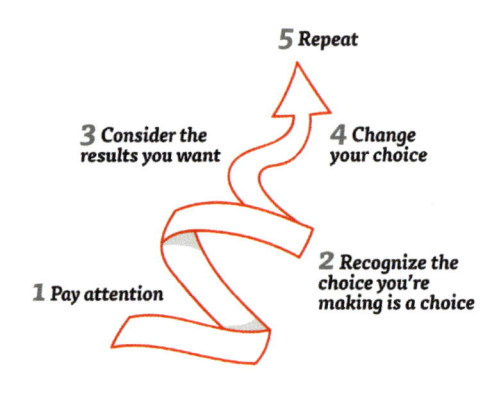

5 Repeat

3 Consider the results you want

4 Change your choice

1 Pay attention

2 Recognize the choice you're making is a choice

WHY DON'T WE REFLECT?

We've noticed whenever we talk about reflecting it's an "easy sell", with lots of nodding and general agreement that reflection is a good thing. We then do an exercise focused on reflection and most people still fail to do it! Given its benefits, it's amazing we don't reflect more. We did some research[61] I'd like to share here, showing the four main reasons people tell us why they don't reflect.

1. It's embarrassing.

We worry about sounding silly or weird - but we shouldn't. People love to talk about themselves and you will only notice the warm glow of being listened to if you do it right.

2. They don't want to let the other person "get away with anything."

I have never understood this response and always ask "What are you letting them away with? All you're doing is listening to them and making sure they felt heard. What's the downside?" I've never heard a satisfactory reply and would love to hear from you if you have one.

3. They worry that the other person will hear their reflection as agreement or aggression.

It isn't. What we say and how we say it is obviously key here. Practice will help, but clearly my saying: "This sounds really important to you," or nodding my head and going "hmm" doesn't mean I'm going to go along with your decision.

4. They already know the answer.

This reason is my favourite. A large percentage of people tell us that they don't reflect as much as they should because they're not really listening, explaining that: "I already know what they're going to say."

No, you don't. You couldn't possibly know what their filters have produced. You could have an idea, but you don't know for sure.

If you want to manage your behaviour and actions, you must manage your emotions. That means giving up the certainty that your Potential is right.

You might be right 99 per cent of the time, but it's still a poor reason not to spend a very small amount of time and energy needed to get all the positives from reflection.

Which one of the reasons here applies to **your** HardTalk?

GETTING BETTER AT LISTENING IS DIFFICULT BUT WORTH IT

It's not just the FBI who value the skills in ListenHard. They're valued everywhere. If you look at the behaviours needed for success in occupations ranging from leadership to psychology to sales, you'll see them. And it's very respectful - it works across all cultures, because everyone wants to be heard.

You can tell you're doing it right because it's exhausting. Listening isn't hard mechanically - it's easy not to speak for example (in fact, you're probably doing it right now!) but it's tough emotionally. The best way of getting better at it is to practice and the best kind of practice is practice with specific, actionable feedback.

This is hard, so we've added a few twists to the usual feedback forms and you can download these via the HardTalk website.

Watch out for adjectives and adverbs

An adjective is a way to embellish a noun, and an adverb is a way to embellish a verb - and both modifiers indicate there might be some emotion behind what the person is saying. Adjectives and adverbs are a way of considering what's going on in a person's brain - you don't see everything clearly, but the shadow may give you a sense of what to ask next.

Adjectives are almost always Potentials - they tell us about a judgement someone has made based on some Truths. We need to stick to the Truths if we are to get any results in HardTalk, so adjectives should prompt us to ask questions.

Which is what we should be doing when listening.

Adverbs also tell us there are Truths to be found, because they tell us how something is perceived, and that can prompt us to ask why.

ADDENDUM: A NOTE OF CAUTION FOR THOSE IN POWER

(That may not be the same as a position of authority)

A note of caution: if you're in a position of power you may find HardTalk even harder. You will certainly find it harder to get honest feedback. Some research suggests that you will struggle to SpeakSoft and to ListenHard with chilling implications for your career and the results you care about, not to mention your well-being, and that of those around you.

A psychology professor at UC Berkeley, Dacher Keltner, found subjects under the influence of power act as if they have suffered a traumatic brain injury as they become less aware of risks, more impulsive and, most importantly, are less adept at seeing things from the point of view of other people[62]. Research by neuroscientist Sukvinder Obhi at McMaster University, Ontario showed this may be because power impacts a specific neural process that is key to empathy.[63]

Mirroring - in neuroscience terms - is a subtle kind of mimicry that goes on entirely within our heads, and without our awareness. When we watch someone perform an action, the part of the brain we would use to do that same thing lights up in sympathetic response. It's what we mean when we say we're experiencing something vicariously.

Obhi used a transcranial-magnetic-stimulation machine, to show the mirroring functions of those operating under the influence of power were diminished, compared to those without.

Other studies have shown that because of what Keltner called the "power paradox", power can make it harder to imagine what it's like to be someone else. A famous experiment in 2006 asked participants to draw the letter E on their foreheads so that others could see it.[64] Those feeling powerful were three times more likely to draw the E so that it made sense to themselves rather than their partner. They also did worse guessing how a colleague might interpret a remark - assuming they had information or insight they didn't, in fact, have (remember the spiders in the Smarties box in Chapter 4) or correctly identifying what someone is feeling when looking at a picture of their face.

> **The Power Paradox[63]:**
>
> *"Once we have power, we lose some of the capacities we needed to gain it in the first place."*
>
> Prof. Dacher Keltner

As we saw earlier, one way we can build empathy with others is to literally mirror their behaviour. This doesn't just make them feel more comfortable - it helps us understand how they are feeling by triggering the same feelings in us. If we smile, or hunch over, we get an insight into what the other person is feeling when they do the same. Powerful people are less likely to do this.

This is true even when the power isn't real - most of the subjects in the studies mentioned here were "triggered" into feeling briefly powerful. So how much more likely is this response when power is something that has been build up over years? When it's sustained and deserved? And what happens to the brain afterwards? What about the empathetic abilities then? Can they rejuvenate?

Knowledge is supposed to be power. But what good is power if, when it comes, it deprives you of knowledge? Is it inevitable?

Firstly, no. It doesn't seem to be inevitable. Power leads individuals (and teams) to screen out information that isn't immediately relevant. This will often help to improve efficiency, but it may lead to us missing information that would make us more effective.

It means that, if we're in a position where we can simply command resources - a "tell and yell" situation, then there's no problem. But if, like most people in developed economies, you rely on taking people with you - them deciding to follow you - rather than just yelling "jump", you might want to work on this.

Powerful people can start to believe they know all the answers. They stop asking questions. They don't really listen, they spend the time thinking about what they are going to say next, and how they are going to phrase it beautifully.

Or, worse, they just keep talking. If only the other person can be made to understand the world in the same way as the clever person in charge, surely, they will change their mind? This will, at some stage in their career, limit not only their growth but that of their team, and probably their business.

As we get more senior we are more likely to be rewarded for the results that come with listening and asking questions, rather than for knowing the right answer. But we need to work hard to remember that. You can't stop being powerful but you can - at least occasionally - stop feeling powerful. Power is not a business card or a budget - it's a state of mind. Remembering a time you did not feel powerful can help your brain get a grip again.

Interestingly, if you've experienced a period of real powerlessness you may have "innoculated" your brain, so even long periods of power later in life won't make you risk-averse. For this to work the earlier period without power has to have been truly awful.

SOME SITUATIONS NEED YOU TO REDUCE YOUR FEELINGS OF POWER MORE THAN OTHERS

If you find yourself in any of these three situations, consider making yourself feel less powerful:

1. *You need to deal with a complex problem*

Yes, of course, you're clever and you've asked questions, but it's not enough. The world is a very complex place and, remember *"unless you're Google, you don't know everything"*. Getting other points of view and seeing the world through a variety of eyes can mean the difference between success and failure.

This is especially difficult if you're in a position of power, because many people may be reluctant to speak up. It's your job to "make" them. You can't do this simply by saying "we have an open-door policy" or setting up a suggestions box.

Instead you must learn to listen hard.

At a minimum, this means learning to stay quiet, to ask great questions, to give people time to answer them and **not** react badly when they speak up. (Hint: "Don't you think we should do XYZ?" is not a good question. It's not even really a question.)

2. You need to develop others

At some stage in your career, (probably much earlier than you think), it's your job to develop others. Think about it: if you don't develop the people below and around you, then who is going to be able to take over your role when you move on?

Being clever is useful here because you will have knowledge that you can pass on. But knowledge isn't enough – you have, over time, built up a way of thinking or schema that is probably so deeply a part of you that you hardly even recognise it any more.

Try reflecting on the questions you ask yourself to define your problems and challenges, and the solutions you create. Then ask your people these questions. They may not always get the "right" answer, but it will help them to build their abilities. You never know, they may even come up with better solutions than you.

3. You need other people to get things done

Unless you have absolute power (and if you do then you really don't need to be reading books like this) then, no matter how great your idea is, you will need others to implement it. That will mean persuading them that the idea is worthwhile, achievable and in their best interest.

You need to understand where they are and what they are thinking. This is why listening skills are a key component of what the FBI teaches its crisis negotiators: they understand that if you want people to change their behaviour, you have to understand why they currently behave differently. Once you understand this, you can then communicate effectively, touching on the facts and emotions that are important to your audience, rather than simply sharing the facts.

People don't make decisions based simply on facts – if they did nobody would smoke or eat food that's bad for them.

There's nothing wrong with being powerful. We need powerful people, but power involves more than simply knowing the right answer. Listening effectively and asking great questions gives you insight into how others think, and can help everyone continue to learn and succeed.

As well as reminding yourself of times when you weren't powerful, you can also work hard to make sure that you stay grounded - emptying the bins, spending time with children who are scathingly honest, going home to your family. Making sure you have people around you outside work who will tell you the truth is important, as is working on all Six Sources of influence (see page 130), to make sure the people around you will speak up.

Whatever you do, don't ListenHard and then, when you get the other person to speak up, punish them for doing so, unless you want to make sure they never speak up again.

> *We once worked with a senior leadership team to help them develop a "safety culture". They defined this as one in which anyone and everyone had a right and an obligation to speak up if they saw anyone (no matter*

> their position in the hierarchy) do something unsafe. This represented a huge change from the status quo, and took some time and energy to achieve.
>
> Eventually, we started to see the needle shift as employees started to believe management when they said they wanted to hear bad news and were given the skills needed to share it. It seemed like we'd "won" when, one day, I was walking with the CEO down a corridor and a relatively lowly employee (a receptionist) came out of an office, interrupting our conversation to say: "I'm so sorry to interrupt, but I know you are interested in safety, and I need your help. There's a hole in the carpet on the stairs and it's very dangerous - especially for ladies in high heels."
>
> The CEO stopped in his tracks, raised his eyebrows, turned his head and said: "See? This is the problem with giving people an inch - they take a mile!"
>
> In that moment, the CEO had undone all the work he and his team had put in over the previous months and years as the story spread like wildfire that speaking up will get you shut down no matter what the "values" on the intranet say!

Listening is the hardest skill in my opinion. You can tell you're doing it right because it's exhausting. If you do it right, people will tell you things you don't like. That's the point. You want to hear everything - good and bad. Maybe particularly bad. That's hard. Because people don't want to speak up. You must Listen VERY hard to make them do that. Responding well to what you hear is part of that. Remember HardTalk might not just involve difficult subjects for your partner, you might find the reaction hard.

YOU CAN HIRE FOR HARDTALK - AND PEOPLE DO

I believe everybody can get better at HardTalk, and it is possible to build a culture where this is more likely. But one "shortcut" to doing this is to hire for candour - or the ability to have difficult conversations.

It's been reported that after interviewing job candidates, hiring managers at Apple filled out a form containing one intriguing question: "Could this person have gone toe-to-toe with Steve Jobs[65]?" Moreover, Arianna Huffington hires people who can do HardTalk and has been quoted as saying: "I love working with people who say exactly what's on their minds[66]".

TRAINING CAN HELP

Training is obviously important too. Our research suggests that people don't feel they have the skills to speak up, and that these can be taught. But that isn't the case, it's been done successfully in the military and in air travel and, to some extent, in healthcare, although greater efforts are necessary here.

Of course, training alone is not enough. It can help to change culture, but it's not capable of changing things alone. That takes a lot more. But it is doable.

HOW HARD YOU TRY WILL DEPEND ON HOW MUCH YOU CARE

Many people want to know how hard they must listen. The unsatisfactory answer is that it depends. To make other people feel like you're listening hard enough that they want to speak is hard work, but if you care about your results then you'll try.

POWER ISN'T JUST BAD FOR LISTENING

Power doesn't just stop you from being able to listen and understand others, it also makes you less likely to behave in a way which endears you to others. SpeakingSoft doesn't come naturally, it seems, to those in power.

A study published in 2013 in the Academy of Management Journal reported that participants triggered to feel powerful yelled and swore more, and they were rude to, or made fun of, co-workers[67]. This makes sense, as power makes us feel special and more deserving of, or entitled to, for example, respect. Perhaps unsurprisingly, the "powerful" also reported feeling their co-workers weren't showing them enough respect. This kind of perception is likely to provoke its own self-confirming data, leading to another spiral you will want to avoid if you want to stay in power and enjoy it.

CHAPTER 7 | 10
ADDENDUM

CHAPTER SUMMARY

- *"Listening is one of the most important aspects to a successful HardTalk. Although we do it every day, we don't usually do it very well. Don't be a 'Topper' or a 'Plusser'"*

- *"The FBI handles the toughest hostage negotiations by working through their behavioural change stairway that focuses on understanding the other fully in order to achieve your Purpose"*

- *"Listen for 3 things to Listen better: Facts, Emotions and Opportunities for questions"*

- *"To successfully ListenHard you must Invite (be curious, stay quiet and encourage) and Reflect (paraphrase, mirror and label)"*

Addendum

- *"Those in power can often find they have become desensitised to the emotions and feelings of others and will need to take more specific action to combat their natural biases"*

- *"Encourage others to speak up without punishment"*

- *"Remember, cultivating a culture where HardTalk can thrive isn't just good for your employees, it is good for your bottom line"*

SUM IT UP

CHAPTER 8

Nothing changes without a conversation and nothing changes after the conversation without accountability. Avoid the ambiguity altogether and don't waste your HardTalk by forgetting to lay out a framework for resolution.

> " ACCOUNTABILITY IS THE GLUE THAT BINDS COMMITMENT TO RESULTS "
>
> Anonymous

PEOPLE CAUSE CONFUSION AND THAT NEEDS TO BE MANAGED

Most businesses are a place of confusion. This is obvious because, mostly, when you put a lot of people together it leads to confusion. That's why we have policies, processes and procedures in place - to deal with people!

The more diversity within a business, the more opportunities for confusion. The more opportunities, too, for creativity and innovation and lots of other great things; but to get there you must first deal with the increased propensity towards confusion. In fact, the need to deal with confusion or potential confusion has infused the whole book. We need to be equally cognizant of these issues at the end of our HardTalk conversation.

The idea of Hardtalk is to get results. The tools and techniques in this book should lead you to a proposed outcome, or set of actions. Making that outcome, or those actions, a reality is what this chapter is all about.

CHAPTER 8
SUM IT UP (FINISHHARD)

People are bad at change, even when it's good for them

Businesses are full of people. People are bad at change. We're bad at doing stuff we know we should - even people who rely on taking medicine to keep them healthy are notoriously bad at remaining faithful to their regime.

Every day we make promises we don't keep. It's why gym membership works as a business model: if everybody who paid for gyms turned up it would be a disaster! It's why so many "great" initiatives aren't actually great at all, insofar as they never really take off and are, eventually, quietly ignored.

We need help to change and to do the right thing. Yet we don't often get or give that help at the end of a HardTalk conversation.

We need to do better by following a simple framework designed to avoid confusion, and make it less likely we will need to have any future HardTalk.

04 FinishHard™

FinishHard™ - setting up the basics of an accountability framework

At this stage, we assume you've used the tools and techniques in this book to work through the specific issue you identified and, if necessary, used the Six Sources to identify barriers beyond personal motivation or ability, as well as solutions. You now have to make sure that that outcome is implemented - that the actions identified because of the conversation actually take place. This means holding people, including yourself, to account.

In every working culture, whatever the individual filters, there's a need to hold people to account. So, this is about doing that in a respectful way.

There are real risks in not completing a HardTalk properly - you will feel you have wasted your time, so you're less likely to try HardTalk in future. You may even resent the person who isn't doing what was "agreed" with implications for your relationship and all that entails.

The FinishHard framework will reduce the risk of this happening.

When we work with existing teams on HardTalk for teams, we develop a Team Charter or written list of behaviours that we will call out - for good or bad. In individual HardTalk scenarios this is also where you, too, set yourself up for success. Like most things in HardTalk the things you must do aren't difficult in themselves. In fact, what you must do is easy...

Define the "WWWWWH", in writing, with your HardTalk partner.

It's just about remembering to do it!

WHO?
WHAT?
WHERE?
WHEN?
WHY?
HOW?

FINISHHARD 144

Define the WWWWWH

The what? The WWWWWH – Who, What, When, Where, Why and How.

If you can get this right, then everybody knows what's expected of them and this is often the (relatively easily solved) problem. Ambiguity can lead to delay or worse, particularly when working across different languages or cultures. You need to be able to answer the following questions (at least):

Who is responsible for the action agreed?
NB: Only one person can be responsible. There may be a need for two or more people to work together and so be accountable, or multiple actions required, but only one person is responsible for each action.

What is this person responsible for?
What verb are they to do?

When are they expected to do it?
This requires a date or referral to other date i.e. before the summer is not helpful nor is after Ramadan.

Where will this take place?
Is there a geographical scope?

Why are we doing this?
What is the expected result or objective?

How will this be done?
Are any resources needed?

Finally how, where and when will we check in on progress?
Simply answering these questions will reduce the likelihood of confusion. Doing so in writing is where the magic starts to happen.

Who is responsible for the action agreed?
NB: Only one person can be responsible. There may be a need for two or more people to work together and so be accountable, or multiple actions required, but only one person is responsible for each action.

What is this person responsible for?
What verb are they to do?

_____
_____
_____

When are they expected to do it?
This requires a date or referral to other date i.e. before the summer is not helpful nor is after Ramadan.

_____
_____
_____

Where will this take place?
Is there a geographical scope?

_____
_____
_____

Why are we doing this?
What is the expected result or objective?

_____
_____
_____

How will this be done?
Are any resources needed?

_____
_____
_____

When are they expected to do it?
This requires a date or referral to other date i.e. before the summer is not helpful nor is after Ramadan.

_____
_____
_____

Finally how, where and when will we check in on progress?
Simply answering these questions will reduce the likelihood of confusion. Doing so in writing is where the magic starts to happen.

_____
_____
_____

YOUR BRAIN DOES NOT WANT TO REMEMBER THINGS - SO WRITE THEM DOWN

We are all very busy. Your brain should be able to spend its time on doing things, not trying to remember things that could be easily stored elsewhere.

This is the premise of a fantastic book called *Getting Things Done* by David Allen[68] where he explains the science behind this. You don't have to use a pen and paper - I use the colour-coded categories on my online calendar in a system that works well for me - but you do need to write it down. Create a system that means you get reminded, rather than having to remember to look at what you're supposed to be doing.

The other reason we write things down is that it's easy to make mistakes/misinterpret things, so we write them down to reduce confusion and stress.

There are real costs associated with the

amount of time and energy spent fixing mistakes that never needed to be made, or dealing with debris from fighting. These costs exist in relatively monolingual and monocultural environments, so those with more diversity must be even more at risk.

This is about setting up a framework for accountability - it's about letting the other party know, clearly, what you want/need and what you and they have agreed to.

You're letting them know how and when they'll be assessed, and how to do a good job. If you can do that everything else gets easier. It's only fair, and it's what everyone wants.

> There is a (probably) apocryphal story about a CEO who calls in a coach to discuss his CFO. The CEO is frustrated and tells the coach that he wishes the CFO would just do what he needs her to do. The coach asks what that is, makes some notes, concludes the session and meets with the CFO. She is equally frustrated, complaining that the CEO won't tell her what he needs from her to really make a difference and seems to be keeping her out of the loop. The coach then shares the list made earlier with the CFO. She, in turn, starts to do the things on them - none of which were impossible, or even difficult, like sending a weekly update on one page and working more closely with three key suppliers.
>
> Success! The moral of the story is clearly that clarity is cool because everybody likes knowing what's expected of them.
>
> PS: The story ends with the CEO refusing to pay the coach because it was "too easy".

FinishingHard: talking it over

This brings us onto the final element of FinishingHard - doing it with the HardTalk partner. We suggest you work with your HardTalk partner to help you best figure out a solution to the issue you've identified as you're more likely to:

- identify actions that will get results
- see the actions implemented
- hold the other person to account if they've come up with the plan

Getting "buy-in" is a phrase we hear a lot, but often it doesn't mean much. In fact, if you'd recently arrived from outer space you'd be forgiven for thinking that "getting buy-in" means "building a set of PowerPoint slides carefully designed to ignore the real issues and clothe everything in a feeling of fait accompli".

Real buy-in is, of course, the opposite.

Getting real buy-in means accepting you may not have all the answers, and asking for the other person to get involved - to hear and be heard.

Don't forget to periodically paraphrase yourself and ask them to do the same, so you can really gauge understanding.

Don't expect everyone to feel comfortable speaking up if there's a problem - you'll still need to ListenHard.

This seems sensible and relatively easy (assuming you've done the HardWork). So why don't people do it? Is there a downside?

WHAT'S THE DOWNSIDE?

I genuinely believe defining the WWWWWH, in writing, with your HardTalk partner would solve a large part of the productivity gap in knowledge workers. Even if it's only marginally effective it would be worth it. But what is the downside?

One potential downside is that you may

not like the solution your HardTalk partner suggests. Of course, you might like it more than something you could have come up with, but you don't have to accept it. If what they're suggesting is flawed in some way, then you need to say so. That's a different HardTalk.

What is the alternative? You can't impose your solutions. Those days are gone. We work in a world of more and more complicated organisational charts, where "command and control" is no longer an option.

We work in a world where our partner might be down the corridor or across an ocean.

We work in a world where our results depend more and more on persuading people (over whose rating and rewards we have little control) to get involved and spend their time, energy and capital (of all kinds) with us.

We work in a world where, even if you have full-time direct reports, the chances are they can simply refuse to do as you say, sabotage you, or just leave, so why set yourself up for failure?

Why not get people involved?

I believe the real reason people don't do this is because there's a conspiracy against accountability and candour. It's hard, and we don't like doing things that are hard. Those who can master these hard skills and do them, despite the discomfort, are likely to be in high demand. You're probably nodding now, but do you really do this?

I often deliver keynotes and seminars around HardTalk. Once, I was with a group of senior professionals - leaders in a large multinational organisation with serious expertise in their field, and track records to prove their value. The topic was delegation, and all went great.

The group were warm and receptive, (I had worked with many of them before), and even when I ribbed them about not identifying the most important reason for delegating* they took it in good humour.

Then I asked them to write down three tasks they would delegate the next day.

The atmosphere changed as they realised this was getting serious. It wasn't just talk. I reassured them they didn't have to share this with anyone and we continued. I then asked the participants to put a name next to the various tasks. At this stage I almost experienced a revolt, as people simply didn't want to do as asked.

I stopped the exercise and we worked through what was going on until, finally, one of the most senior guys said, "I think we might have chosen the wrong topic to focus on - our problem seems more like an accountability thing, rather than delegating."

This was the moment that team started to really begin the HardWork needed as individuals and a group to move towards a culture of candour where HardTalk is not just expected, but facilitated and rewarded. Being able to "discuss the undiscussable" is always a valuable leadership skill.

THE PEN IS MIGHTIER THAN THE COMPLAINT

Many of the people who ask us for help with HardTalk start by telling us they have no power. If you have no power, then defining the WWWWWH in writing should be your first step.

When I work in an organisation I have no power. I am the lowest of the low. I'm an

*The most important reason for delegating is the one most people never think of - the other person might be better at the task than you are!

external supplier. It's my job to make the person who hired me look good, and often to say things nobody else wants to. Everybody knows I will eventually be going, and I'm often very unpopular for some of my time in any organisation. Some people (not many I hope!) remain less than fans long after I leave.

This is because, by definition, I'm there to bring change. But I have no power in the sense that we usually mean the word.

Beyond relying on the power of my sponsor, I rely on writing things down and it works. The simple act of having somebody commit to a task and a system to follow up and then holding them to this commitment can work marvels.

> We had been developing and facilitating several offsites working with a new CEO in a GCC semi-governmental organisation to bring about a change in culture. Each offsite ended with a list of actions and names against them as per the FinishHard framework. The participants were expected to then complete these and be ready to review at the next offsite. In the meantime, I would be working with a different group, jumping out intermittently to do the follow up as agreed. And so, the carousel continued.
>
> One day, three months into the engagement, I walked into the CEO's office. He looked up, smiled and said, "I should have guessed you were coming in today." I must have looked confused as he explained: "People were running around doing things so I'm guessing today is a follow up day?" He had noticed a pattern - the people who had tasks to do would ignore them until they realised that I really was going to ask them to explain what had happened, and come up with a plan to make sure everyone did as they had promised.
>
> I had no power beyond the skills in this book.

If, for example, you're working on a project with a weak leader and no culture of self-accountability within the team, try using my technique of writing things down as a structure for meetings.

If you work with volunteers, or in another situation where you have no authority, get people to sign off on using this.

It's respectful, helpful to you and the other person/people in managing time and effort. In the worst-case scenario, it provides metrics against which you can build some Truths - the basis of all HardTalk.

> *If you're worried about holding others accountable, don't be. Not only is it a skill you must develop if you're to be useful to any organisation, it's also a skill other human beings will value in you.*
>
> *As I was writing this chapter my phone rang. It was a coaching client who is in the process of preparing his case for a big promotion. He'd sent me a "script" he'd been working on and was calling to discuss it. I started the conversation by saying: "So you've been busy," as he was 24 hours late in sending me the document.*
>
> *He laughed and agreed that he had come into the office early because he knew I was waiting for it and would hold him accountable. This sensible, ambitious, disciplined man wanted, in fact, needed, someone to make sure he completed the forms necessary for his promotion. Crazy but true!*

CHAPTER SUMMARY 8

- *"The more diverse your organisation is, the more you will need to manage potential confusion, yours and theirs"*

- *"Even if you have done all the HardTalk steps right, you will 'fail' at your Talk if you don't FinishHard by clarifying with your partner what the agreed outcome is"*

- *"Define the WWWWWH: Who, What, When, Where, Why and How"*

- *"An agreed WWWWWH with your HardTalk partner will: identify actions that will get results, see the actions implemented and hold the person responsible to account"*

- *"If possible, write your conclusions down and share it with each other. This record and reminder will combat our brains natural ability to forget things we shouldn't"*

- *"The WWWWWH works particularly well in situations where you might feel as though you have less power than your HardTalk partner. An agreed course of action is easier to refer too when chasing the right results."*

WHAT IF?

CHAPTER 9

Curiosity is crucial. Never stop asking questions. HardTalk is called Hard for a reason – we answer the questions that matter, so you can have your best HardTalk.

> "CURIOSITY. IT KEEPS US MOVING FORWARD, EXPLORING, EXPERIMENTING, OPENING NEW DOORS"
>
> Walt Disney

As we've talked to clients and delivered the HardTalk workshop, we've noticed some questions/concerns coming up repeatedly. We address these here, and suggest you approach them with one overarching thought: which of the BrainDrains is at play here?

In other words, are you sure your brain isn't working against you, allowing you to react rather than to respond? To focus on the short-term "feel good now" objectives rather than your healthy, "feel good in the longer term" Purpose?

Is the premise behind your question based on Truths or have your filters blinded you?

The number one question we hear is:

What if I don't want to learn to say things more nicely?

You don't have to. This programme is not about saying bad things in a nice way. It's not about being nice to others. It's not "soft" skills. It's about results. It's based on solid research and, if implemented, the behaviours you learn will get you closer to the results you want. It's not a magic bullet. It's called HardTalk because it's Hard. It's not easy for you or your HardTalk partner in the short-term, but it's the right thing in the medium and long-term. And it gets easier.

Another frequently heard question is:

What if my boss is a bully?

Bullies exist. Often people who behave in a bullying fashion score high on the Social Dominance Orientation (SDO) Test (available to HardTalk members via the website). These are the people who see the world as "winner takes all" where, unless you are "above" them in some way, respect is not due.

It doesn't matter if your boss is a bully. Or an idiot. Or your HardTalk partner reports into another region. You always have **two options:**

- do nothing
- do something

with five possible outcomes:

OUTCOMES

- do nothing and be miserable
- do nothing and make that your decision and focus on something else
- do something and run a risk and see things get better
- do something and run a risk and see things stay the same
- do something and run a risk and see things get worse

Because HardTalk follows the Rules of Adulting, you never have to have HardTalk. But if you don't have it, you must live with the consequences - ideally without making things worse!

Let's start with this - all else being equal, It's your job to speak up. If you don't have anything to say, then find somewhere you can contribute. If you're not speaking up because you're being squashed, then you should be speaking about that, or thinking about how to leave - why would you want to work somewhere that isn't interested in you and what you have to say?

That doesn't mean you get to have your own way all the time. Sometimes the decision won't go your way, and there really might be nothing you can do. At that moment, you must decide to get on board and work with the decision, or let it go and leave!

Don't be the person who's always negative, gossiping and plotting. That person isn't good for creativity, innovation or fun. If you're that person - stop it. Because nobody likes people who complain all the time and don't do anything to change it. People who hold grudges and are negative sap energy, reduce productivity and cause unnecessary stress. They are toxic for teams and organisations.

Evil does exist (although it's a lot less prevalent than simple incompetence) but even when the HardTalk partner you have is "bad", you still need to find ways to influence them.

You can use the Six Sources framework to help with that, but a good start is always the Platinum Rule: "Treat people as they want to be treated". What does a boss with high Social Dominance Orientation (SDO) want? What do they value?

As a rule, people with high SDO want to know you "get it"; that you understand they're important, so go out of your way to show you respect their position on the hierarchy. This might be done by 'sharing the spotlight' with the boss, acknowledging both publicly and privately the instrumental role the boss played in your accomplishments.

You might also share with your supervisor any additional resources you enjoy because of their performance. Consider contrasting up front to deal with any potential confusion about your Purpose.

What if I know my potential is right?

Some people will have read through this book shaking their heads and thinking "but not in my case". They are thinking of a HardTalk scenario they know about, and separating the Truths from the Potentials all while thinking: "Yes, but I know why this person does that - they're lazy and disorganised and know they can get away with it because their brother is the CEO!".

Maybe they're right!

But this isn't about being right. This is about getting what you want. That means changing your action, controlling your emotions and allowing for different interpretations. This control is key to managing your actions. It's about managing your actions and behaviour even when the other person makes it hard. Even when they are not behaving well.

You still get to think and to say the Potential you think is mostly likely to be correct, and you still get to act on it. But firstly, you recognise there are alternative interpretations. This means you're less likely to be fooled into reacting badly.

It's not about being right - you might be right - it's about kicking your brain into gear - it's about self-awareness and self-control.

This is called reappraisal - a cognitive behavioural therapy technique that helps you see tough situations in new ways.

Reappraisal

When volunteers were confronted by angry faces and told to feel the emotion on the face and think about what it meant, they continued to be upset. But when instructed to imagine that the face's bearer was having a bad day, they were like Teflon - the bad feeling didn't stick and in FMRI brain scans, the reappraisers' brains look healthier.

What if I'm wrong?

It's ok if your potential is wrong because you're entering the HardTalk knowing that might be the case. This means your language (actual and body) and general tone will be respectful. Your awareness that your HardTalk partner may interpret the Truths very differently means you are opening to hearing as well as being heard.

What if I really can't do anything?

This question is usually about an organisational culture or, more rarely, process. Or it's about a person whose displeasure is feared. For now, I want to look at this from the point of view of an organisational culture or process.

This is about "how things are done" and this question implies it can't be changed, not without certain dire consequences. Actually, we know in most cases that's not true. Because things do change, in some places, sometimes. It's never because of nobody speaking out. It's rarely easy. So, it's back to the two options with five possible outcomes.

What if the other person is out to get me?

Are they really? How do you know? Are you being reasonable or are your filters getting in the way? Can you get more data? Remember you still get to decide you don't want to have the conversation - we just want to make sure you are making the decision, and not your monkey brain!

What if the other person doesn't want to talk?

Most people won't. Almost by definition - that's why being able to do this is so effective! It's your job to make them want to. You'll put in just as much effort as the result you want dictates. It's about results and respect.

It's up to you. You have to work as hard as it takes to get them to speak. If you really care, then you'll make it happen. If you don't, you'll give up.

What if my HardTalk partner goes crazy?

How likely is this? You must measure risk and reward. If you decide to go ahead, do we think anything in particular here is likely to set them off? What skills or BrainTrains can you use?

What if you don't have any power?

Power, official power, is over-rated. If you find yourself relying on your position, the title on your card, then you've really lost the game. That's not to say you should never use your power - you can, and you should - but it should be the last resort.

Before you get there, use the Six Sources on page 130 and share the consequences you believe your HardTalk partner faces if the issue you've identified continues. That's more likely to provoke lasting change.

What if it doesn't work?

It might not. It's not a magic bullet and it depends what you mean by "work". You may not get 100 per cent of what you want in one conversation. You will need to practice. You need to be sincere and realistic.

What if it's not my fault?

So what? Do you care about the results?
If so, then the fault doesn't matter.

What if some of my "filters" make HardTalk particularly difficult?

They are likely to. Some 50 per cent of the global population, for example, is socialised to some extent to be quiet and not speak up.[69] Certain cultures also draw the line in different places between deference and respect. This doesn't mean you can't have HardTalk - you need to WorkHard to manage those filters and you also have to respect the filters of others - for example, in the language you use.

What if my HardTalk partner is mean or aggressive in the HardTalk?

That's their decision. You get to decide how you deal with it. Are you going to reciprocate or focus on your Purpose? Can you keep Spock engaged and Homer at bay? Can you remember how you need to "turn up" to get the results you want?

What if it's a busy time of year? Do I still have to have HardTalk?

Yes. Or no. How long could a conversation possibly take? If it's important enough to mention ever, then it's important enough to bring up when it's fresh and before it festers.

"Ironically, people who suppress the mini-confrontations for fear of conflict tend to have huge conflicts later, which can lead to separation, precisely because they let minor problems fester. On the other hand, people who address the mini-conflicts head-on in order to straighten things out tend to have the great, long-lasting relationships."

— Ray Dalio[70], Billionaire Investor

What if I want to do my HardTalk through SMS? Email?

Do you really have to? Honestly? Why? Are you really just avoiding it? Please don't have your HardTalk via SMS or email. Trust us, it isn't worth the confusion and misunderstanding and you'll just end up having to have more HardTalks!

What if it's someone powerful I need to have HardTalk with?

Your HardTalk partner is, by definition, someone you care about for some reason. You might like them, be related, or have to work with them, but if there's no relationship there's unlikely to be HardTalk. So, whoever it is, you must make the decision. Remember everyone is fundamentally the same, really, and the HardTalk approach is respectful - you are asking to be heard and to hear others.

What if it's someone close to me?

See above.

What if they hold a grudge?

See above.

What if the repercussions are worse than not having the HardTalk?

Then don't do it! But remember it's not just the severity of the repercussions you need to consider. It's the severity of the repercussions multiplied by the likelihood of the repercussions actually taking place. And we're doom-mongers. You might be overestimating this.

What if it's too hard?

No one can answer this question for you, because no one else knows how important the issue at stake is. That's why the first thing we do is work through the questions in the Decision Tree as we did in the Introduction to decide whether to have the conversation at all.

Remember, you can download the DecisionTree at **www.hardtalk.info**

What if it doesn't work the first time?

It might not. Like everything difficult, we can't always get it right the first time, but keep trying and we promise it will be worth it.

The lack of immediate success is a mixture of HardTalk being, by its nature, difficult, and often about issues that have been "festering" for a while.

We are talking about putting into practice a set of skills and, as we'll see in the next Chapter, developing skills is a process that takes time.

CHAPTER SUMMARY

- *"This programme isn't about finding a way to be nicer. It is about getting lasting results"*

- *"There could be lots of reasons you don't want to have your HardTalk, maybe they are even good ones, but you must weigh them against the consequences of not speaking up, which can often be dire"*

- *"Your HardTalk partner might be aggressive or mean or domineering, but there are always filters to explain their behaviour. Try to consider those possibilities and how to manage them when approaching your HardTalk"*

- *"HardTalk, when done properly, can be very effective, even with those you might consider more 'powerful' than you"*

- *"HardTalk should always be done face to face – this will reduce the potential for confusion or misinterpretation"*

- *"It might not work perfectly the first time, especially as it is difficult, but it will be worth the effort"*

MAKE IT STICK

CHAPTER 10

Usually it isn't easy to put new learning into practice. But HardTalk training has been designed to 'stick' so it becomes part of our instinctive behaviour. Using neuroscientific techniques and research, you can climb the ladder of learning and always be ready for a successful HardTalk.

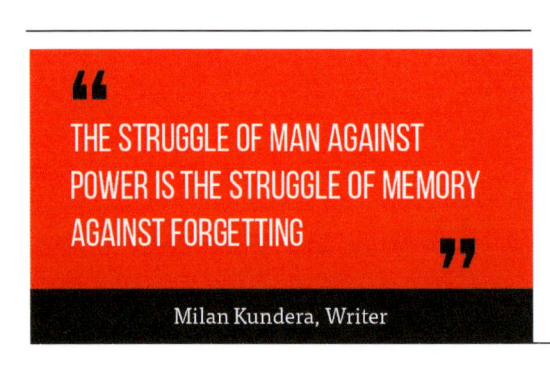

> **THE STRUGGLE OF MAN AGAINST POWER IS THE STRUGGLE OF MEMORY AGAINST FORGETTING**
>
> Milan Kundera, Writer

It's hard to learn new skills and embed them so they become "natural". When we want to get better at a skill it takes time - we spend time rehearsing musical instruments, practicing moves in sport, talking in a foreign language. It's the same for HardTalk and we know we need to do this to move up the *Ladder of Learning*.

It's hard to get out of bad habits and into good ones - if it wasn't, nobody would smoke, and nobody would be overweight.

We're bad at doing the things we should do in daily life if the results aren't immediate. We're set up to focus on the short-term.

Ladder of Learning

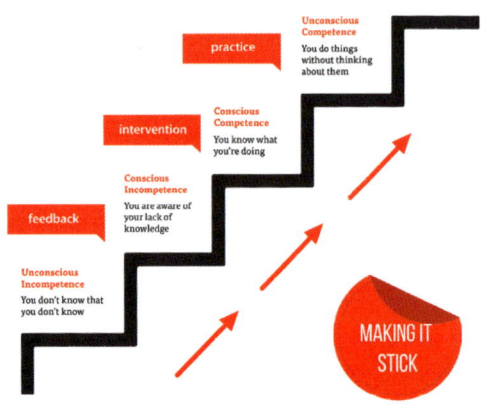

- **feedback** — Unconscious Incompetence: You don't know that you don't know
- Conscious Incompetence: You are aware of your lack of knowledge
- **intervention** — Conscious Competence: You know what you're doing
- **practice** — Unconscious Competence: You do things without thinking about them

MAKING IT STICK

CHAPTER 10

MAKE IT STICK

Reading books like this, doing the exercises and even attending HardTalk training will only take you so far.

For that reason, we've used tips from neuroscientists, and others who research how we learn, to incorporate strategies designed to help us move up the Ladder of Learning to unconscious competence or "expert" level.

In fact, even the design of this book incorporates these strategies, as does the HardTalk programme.

Here you'll see the Make it Stick stages of the blended modular HardTalk programme including the five face-to-face "events" and online exercises designed to maximise retention:

PREPARE

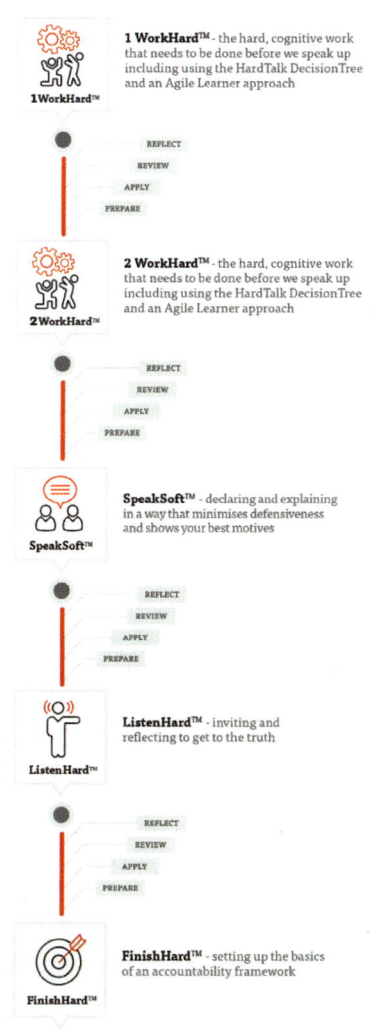

1 WorkHard™ - the hard, cognitive work that needs to be done before we speak up including using the HardTalk DecisionTree and an Agile Learner approach

REFLECT
REVIEW
APPLY
PREPARE

2 WorkHard™ - the hard, cognitive work that needs to be done before we speak up including using the HardTalk DecisionTree and an Agile Learner approach

REFLECT
REVIEW
APPLY
PREPARE

SpeakSoft™ - declaring and explaining in a way that minimises defensiveness and shows your best motives

REFLECT
REVIEW
APPLY
PREPARE

ListenHard™ - inviting and reflecting to get to the truth

REFLECT
REVIEW
APPLY
PREPARE

FinishHard™ - setting up the basics of an accountability framework

COMPLETE

If you stand in front of people, as we do, and show them the "forgetting curve" proposed by Ebbinghaus, you will always get audience reaction as they nod their heads and tell the person next to them that it's true. They've noticed that people take training courses, but nothing much changes in their daily work life as a result.

> **Forgetting curve**[71]
>
> The forgetting curve hypothesizes the decline of memory retention in time. This curve shows how information is lost over time when there is no attempt to retain it. A typical graph of the forgetting curve purports to show that humans tend to halve their memory of newly learned knowledge in a matter of days or weeks unless they consciously review the learned material.

But if behaviour isn't changed, what's the point of a training course (unless it's to provide a nice buffet lunch and maybe a bit of "cross-silo networking")? Or, indeed, what's the point of reading a book like this if nothing changes as a result?

Sometimes training isn't the answer
(Or, at least, the whole answer)

Training is necessary but not sufficient.

Before we deliver any kind of HardTalk training in organisations we conduct a "HardTalk audit", using a framework that builds on the Six Sources of influence.

The idea is to identify any pockets of exceptional practice, as well as support for the HardTalk ethos, and any potential barriers to success.

We've discovered that if senior leadership is not behind the programme, its effectiveness is diminished. Likewise, certain organisational cultures seem to be more difficult to introduce HardTalk to. These cultures suffer from "adherence climates" - where people are expected to follow process mindlessly without ever pointing out flaws or opportunities.

We've found HardTalk to work particularly well in environments where senior leadership has recognised that "network judgement climates" lead to higher performing individuals, teams and organisations and want to ensure the systems and skills are in place to support this.

"We don't know what the future holds, so the most important skill we can develop is the ability to develop new skills."
— Dawn Metcalfe

Research shows that network judgement climates perform 50 per cent better than the adherence climate, with risk of error reduced by 25 per cent.[72] The authors suggest this is because in an increasingly complex world it's nigh on impossible to provide people with a script or checklist for every possible situation. Instead, it makes more sense to empower them to leverage their peers' wisdom, experience, and lessons learned.

> *Network judgment climates are environments in which individuals rely more on advice and guidance from colleagues to inform their own decisions than they do on their own personal experience (individual judgement climates) or on company policies and procedures (adherence climates)*

CHAPTER 10

MAKE IT STICK

Empowerment isn't something that just happens though. It needs senior leadership to support it and to remove any and all barriers to success.

> A regional company wanted to do some HardTalk training. We asked the same first question we always ask: "Who is the training for, and why?" The answer was that the call centre team weren't communicating well, leading to missed objectives and unhappy customers. Clearly, they needed training.
>
> We asked a few more questions and then went to interview some of these people who, during their lives, had apparently never learned to communicate effectively with others.
>
> We asked them why they didn't just follow common sense procedures and take ownership of the customer's issue. It turned out they couldn't. The call centre team couldn't call out. They weren't avoiding confrontation with either the engineers or the customers - they simply didn't have the tools needed to share bad news or to hold others accountable! We worked with the senior leadership with the intention of rolling it out across the organisation, once these barriers to success had been removed.

We want to make sure people who spend their time and money on HardTalk training can actually benefit from it. A HardTalk culture comes from training, but not from training alone. It's also about physical and metaphorical infrastructure, management ethos, leadership, hiring, and a lot more factors. To make sure the training "sticks", we work with companies beforehand to make sure the ground is fertile.

However, although seeds will grow best in fertile ground, they can grow anywhere. If you're an individual who has read this book, or the only person in your team or department who has attended a HardTalk training course, the tools and techniques here, if practiced consistently, can make a huge difference on your interaction with others.

> *"Most of the problems in your life are due to two reasons: you act without thinking, you think without acting."*
>
> — Anonymous

Join the conversation

The art of conversation is like any art – with continued practice you acquire skill and ease. But practicing isn't enough - it needs to be reflective. You need to consider what you did well and what you would change in the future. This requires feedback: specific examples of when a behaviour was observed, or could have been better used.

If you've attended a HardTalk programme, you will have had lots of feedback in the session.

Participants also have access to an online platform where they can:

- complete written tests and other exercises
- use the Rehearsal platform to video themselves using the HardTalk skills
- get feedback from their HardTalk coach and others

In fact, it's so important, we make it a prerequisite of the programme that participants do this before they are certified HardTalkers.

But even if you haven't attended the HardTalk training, don't feel alone, we can help you

MAKE IT STICK 160

move up the Ladder of Learning.

**On the HardTalk website
www.hardtalk.info you can:**

- complete a HardTalk readiness quiz
- access research
- read articles
- ask questions
- download resources
- sign up for HardTalking Insights

(We promise never to spam you and to keep your data private.)

You can also improve the feedback you receive by downloading our unique HardTalk Feedback forms.

Just remember to:

- *note down what you hear*
- *ask for examples/clarifications*
- *say thank you*
- *consider incorporating the feedback into your second "take"*

If your purpose is to learn - to hear and be heard - then your behaviour is automatically better. When somebody approaches you with feedback and you want to hear, you're more likely to react well and get more feedback.

If you can't find anyone you trust to ask to give you feedback, then do it by yourself. Allow yourself the time to think about the different skills or behaviours you want to improve and:

1. Make notes about what you intended to do, what you did, what went well and what you could have improved.

"Nothing so much assists learning as writing down what we wish to remember."
— Marcus Tullius Cicero, Roman Politician

2. Teach others - if you can't, then you don't understand it well. Teaching forces us to be systematic and to know the answers! It also makes it easier for us to behave well, by reminding us we're a role model and so need to walk the talk.
3. Get in a routine - set reminders to review particular skills.
4. Be reasonable - start small. Focus on one skill, and don't start with the most important conversation in your life!

I'm going to leave you with one final thought.

You are just your behaviours to other people. That's all they see. So you must be well-behaved, which means being self-possessed. Learning to remain self-possessed is a lot of effort, but so is studying law or engineering, or getting great at the guitar, or whatever you had to do to build the skills you have now.

HardTalk skills are just as important, because whatever happens in the future you're going to need to get things done with, and through, others, and you're going to have to be able to learn new skills.

Conversely, all you see are behaviours. You're not in the other person's head and don't know for sure what's going on with them. Be humble in your judgements and recognise them as Potentials.

Good luck and stay in touch!

CHAPTER SUMMARY 10

- *"The key to having successful HardTalk is for the new skills you have learnt to become embedded and 'natural' so they become instinctive, even in stressful situations; we need this to move up the Ladder of Learning"*

- *"The HardTalk Handbook and blended training programme have been designed using neuroscience techniques and research to be 'sticky'; to maximise your retention and provide a resource you can visit again and again"*

- *"Successful HardTalk will only thrive in the right culture. A HardTalk audit of your organisation can determine the gaps in your culture that could prevent a culture of candour"*

- *"Network judgement climates (where individuals rely more on advice from colleagues for decisions) perform 50% better than adherence climates (where they rely on company policies more) or individual judgment climates (where they rely on their own personal experience more)"*

- *"Ask for feedback as you practice – we consistently perform better when we feel we are being watched. Even imagining we are being evaluated can make you consider your actions more"*

THE HANDBOOK IN SUMMARY

1

Natural instincts aren't always a friend to us. *In HardTalk they often work directly against our own interests. Understanding our gut reactions better will guide us to determine when we should speak up and when we should let it go.*

2

Emotions are inevitable. *The more you pretend otherwise, the more you're at their mercy. We must learn how to control our emotions, so we can manage our behaviour in HardTalk scenarios.*

3

Patterns are dangerous. *Not wallpaper ones of course, but the ones our lazy brains love to use to create shortcuts. Our brains are filled with these shortcuts and biases, that we aren't even aware of, and they cause us to make costly mistakes.*

4

Understanding the other person *is crucial to knowing how to make sure you are correctly interpreted. Do to this you need to build empathy, trust and understanding in a quick and ethical way.*

5

Your Purpose is what you really want *in the long-term. Your perceived Purpose is what your behaviour suggests you want. You won't succeed if they stay separate..... get aligned.*

6

Your organisation needs you to speak up. *Even if you have a difficult boss, or work in a political environment. Using the 'Declare-Explain' framework, you can talk about pretty much anything.*

7

Listening is fundamental to good communication. *Being misunderstood is toxic to performance and HardTalk. When you Invite and Reflect you can build trust with the other person and get the results you want.*

8

Nothing changes without a conversation *and nothing changes after the conversation without accountability. Avoid the ambiguity altogether and don't waste your HardTalk by forgetting to lay out a framework for resolution.*

9

Curiosity is crucial. *Never stop asking questions. HardTalk is called Hard for a reason – we answer the questions that matter, so you can have your best HardTalk.*

10

Usually it isn't easy to put new learning into practice. *But HardTalk training has been designed to 'stick' so it becomes part of our instinctive behaviour. Using neuroscientific techniques and research, you can climb the ladder of learning and always be ready for a successful HardTalk.*

ACKNOWLEDGEMENTS

"Feeling gratitude and not expressing it is like wrapping a present and not giving it."
— William Arthur Ward One of America's most quoted writers of inspirational maxims

Writing a book is not fun. Even if you're doing it in a beautiful place like Sri Lanka which is where I was fortunate enough to write this. Even if it's a subject you care about. Even with supportive people. Writing a book is a slog and it's work that you've imposed on yourself. But it is easier with supportive people and I've been lucky to have a lot of them. I'm going to try to name names here but I know I'll have forgotten some people - please forgive me.

First, I'd like to say thanks to all the people on social media who stayed with me during summer 2017, keeping me sane as I sat for long stretches on my own, on an island within an island. Some of these are real people whom I now know in "real life" and others are still faceless (to me!).

I also need to thank many organisations in the ever-growing, ever-more-connected business world of Dubai, and the wider Gulf, for their support as clients or partners. The people working for these organisations also played a huge part in this book. Many of the stories here come from them, when they shared their experiences and expertise in training courses or during coaching sessions, through completing research, or just over a cup of coffee. Obviously, all identifying details have been changed.

I am fortunate to be part of an eco-system in Dubai that helped me from the moment I started my business - sharing knowledge, contacts, advice and giving support and useful feedback. It's not a perfect place (where is), but it has many strengths, and one of these is its diversity. I hope to help, in some small way, to harness that diversity by codifying the behaviours I've seen in the most effective communicators in a region where communication is not easy.

But Dubai is not the whole world. Much of the research I rely on in HardTalk comes from researchers and academics across the world. I'd like to thank them for the hard work they do and hope that they'll tell me if I'm not doing them justice. There are literally too many to mention and so I'll just mention one, Professor Art Kohn, whose work very much influenced the development of the programme.

Some other people whose help in developing HardTalk as a programme and as a book deserve special mention include (in no particular order) Fiona Du Vivier, Will Rankin, Oliver Caviglioi, Kateryna Trysh, Satsiri Winberg, Simon Clough, Sarah Jaimie Bahar and Claire Sharrock. They are truly "Team HardTalk" and I appreciate every effort along the way.

Less "technically" useful but still hugely supportive in more personal ways - Amanda Line, Sophie Le Ray, Matt Santaspirt, Paul Pelletier, Steve Harrison, Nick Fisher, Farah Fostouk, Charlie Scott, Guy Guillemard, Megha Merani, Shahjahan Madampat and Giovanni Everduin.

I'd also like to thank the many people who agreed to review the book and help shape it along the way - their names can be seen at the front.

And lastly to the many, many others who I certainly don't mean to insult but can't remember now because I'm tired and it's been a long journey! I thank every single one of you - even if what you did was small it may have happened on a day when some small good thing was all I needed. So thank you. And if what you did was big thank you even more!

The focus of this book and the HardTalk programme is professional HardTalk: the difficult conversations we (should) have in the workplace. But inevitably, an interest in one part of one's life bleeds into another: my family has had to put up with me practicing for years. I love them and thank them for all their help not just in the last year but over my entire life. I have wings because they gave me roots.

REFERENCES

Preface

1. https://www.nytimes.com/2016/02/28/magazine/what-google-learned-from-its-quest-to-build-the-perfect-team.html
2. How Can Decision Making Be Improved?, Perspectives on Psychological Science, Vol 4, Issue 4, 2009 p. 379
3. http://www.businessinsider.com/nicholas-carlson-interviews-facebook-exec-carolyn-everson-2015-12
4. https://www.aacn.org/nursing-excellence/healthy-work-environments/~/media/aacn-website/nursing-excellence/healthy-work-environment/silencekills.pdf?la=en]

Introduction

5. https://en.wikipedia.org/wiki/Stanford_marshmallow_experiment
6. https://www.goodreads.com/author/show/657773.Jim_Rohn
7. https://www.ncbi.nlm.nih.gov/pubmed/23063236

Chapter 1

8. The New Executive Brain: Frontal Lobes in a Complex World, Elkhonon Goldberg, OUP, 2009, ISBN 9780195329407
9. https://www.psychologytoday.com/blog/the-athletes-way/201412/can-reading-fictional-story-make-you-more-empathetic
10. https://www.authentichappiness.sas.upenn.edu/newsletters/authentichappinesscoaching/curiosity
11. https://www.behavioraleconomics.com/mini-encyclopedia-of-be/loss-aversion/
12. https://www.sciencedirect.com/science/article/pii/S0747563213000800
13. http://www2.padi.com/blog/2017/05/04/18-things-dangerous-sharks/
14. http://hardtalk.info/how-our-biases-affect-our-choices/
15. https://www.thecut.com/2015/10/rudeness-in-hospitals-could-kill-patients.html
16. https://en.wikipedia.org/wiki/Patrick_Lencioni

Chapter 2

17. On the Improvement of the Understanding By Benedict de Spinoza p248
18. https://hms.harvard.edu/news/harvard-medicine/anger-management
19. https://hms.harvard.edu/news/harvard-medicine/anger-management
20. The Metaethics of Constitutional Adjudication By Bosko Tripkovic p158
21. https://englishlegalhistory.wordpress.com/2013/06/10/history-of-trial-by-jury/
22. https://www.theguardian.com/science/2014/aug/06/brain-subliminally-

judges-trustworthiness-faces
23. https://www.amazon.com/dp/B0169ATL8G/ref=dp-kindle-redirect?_encoding=UTF8&btkr=1
24. https://www.researchgate.net/publication/26803752_RAGE_Control_Regulate_and_Gain_Emotional_Control
25. https://www.penguinrandomhouse.com/books/316682/why-we-snap-by-r-douglas-fields/9780525954835/
26. http://www.independent.co.uk/arts-entertainment/books/features/extract-nudge-by-richard-h-thaler-amp-cass-r-sunstein-1650321.html
27. https://link.springer.com/chapter/10.1007/978-0-387-89676-2_31

Chapter 3

28. https://www.psychologistworld.com/behavior/pavlov-dogs-classical-conditioning
29. https://www.theguardian.com/women-in-leadership/2013/oct/14/blind-auditions-orchestras-gender-bias
30. http://amosyang.net/wp-content/uploads/2012/11/physicalappearanceandwages.pdf
31. https://faculty.fuqua.duke.edu/~charvey/Research/Working_Papers/W101_A_corporate_beauty.pdf
32. https://ctl.yale.edu/sites/default/files/basic-page-supplementary-materials-files/science_facultys_subtle_gender_biases_favor_male_students.pdf
33. https://www.tolerance.org/professional-development/test-yourself-for-hidden-bias
34. Heidi Grant Halverson & David Rock, 'Beyond Bias', published in Strategy+Business, Autumn 2015 https://www.strategy-business.com/article/00345?gko=d11ee
35. https://www.sciencedirect.com/science/article/pii/S0022103115000396
36. https://insight.kellogg.northwestern.edu/article/better_decisions_through_diversity
37. http://www.nytimes.com/2011/11/27/books/review/thinking-fast-and-slow-by-daniel-kahneman-book-review.html
38. http://www.independent.co.uk/news/business/analysis-and-features/the-moment-it-all-went-wrong-for-kodak-6292212.html
39. http://www.businessinsider.com/how-google-gets-employees-to-eat-healthy-2014-11
40. https://www.networkworld.com/article/2268096/servers/the-downfall-of-sun-microsystems.html
41. https://www.ft.com/content/b8c66e50-beda-11e5-9fdb-87b8d15baec2
42. https://en.wikipedia.org/wiki/Katharine_Birbalsingh
43. https://youtu.be/Bq_xYSOZrgU
44. https://www.inc.com/minda-zetlin/heres-why-bosses-at-google-are-not-allowed-to-hire-fire-or-promote-employees.html

Chapter 4

45. https://en.wikipedia.org/wiki/Theory_of_mind
46. https://www.youtube.com/watch?v=41jSdOQQpv0
47. https://www.ncbi.nlm.nih.gov/pmc/articles/PMC4791048/

Chapter 5

48. https://www.nytimes.com/2016/02/28/magazine/what-google-learned-from-its-

quest-to-build-the-perfect-team.html?_r=0
49. https://en.wikipedia.org/wiki/Patrick_Lencioni
50. https://hbr.org/2016/01/collaborative-overload
51. http://www.fivebehaviors.com/About.aspx
52. https://tinyurl.com/ycvg4u3n
53. http://thebehavioralfinanceguy.com/wp-content/uploads/2017/09/Why-Teams-Dont-Work.pdf
54. http://hardtalk.info/want-to-apologise-properly-be-a-panda/

Chapter 6

55. Letitia Baldrige was an American etiquette expert, public relations executive and author who was most famous for serving as Jacqueline Kennedy's Social Secretary.
56. https://hbr.org/2013/04/the-sandwich-approach-undermin

Chapter 7

57. Bryant McGill is an American author, speaker and activist in the fields of self-development, personal freedom and human rights.
58. https://www.authentichappiness.sas.upenn.edu/newsletters/authentichappinesscoaching/curiosity
59. http://sourcesofinsight.com/six-sources-of-influence/
60. https://www.forbes.com/sites/davidburkus/2015/07/02/the-real-reason-google-serves-all-that-free-food/
61. http://hardtalk.info/research/

Addendum Notes:

62. http://www.independent.co.uk/life-style/powerful-people-brain-injury-traumatic-empathy-mirroring-keltner-study-science-a7807946.html
63. https://www.theatlantic.com/magazine/archive/2017/07/power-causes-brain-damage/528711/
64. http://www.telegraph.co.uk/journalists/daniel-h-pink/8641925/Daniel-H.-Pink-Why-bosses-need-to-show-their-soft-side.html
65. https://www.inc.com/carmine-gallo/steve-jobs-demanded-fearless-feedback-and-so-should-you.html
66. http://www.businessinsider.com/arianna-huffington-qualities-new-hires-2016-12
67. https://www.businessnewsdaily.com/5224-your-ego-may-be-killing-your-workers-performance.html

Chapter 8

68. www.gettingthingsdone.com

Chapter 9

69. The Confidence Code: The Art and Science of Self-Assurance – What Women Should Know (HarperBusiness, 2014)
70. Raymond Dalio is an American investor, hedge fund manager, and philanthropist.

Chapter 10

71. https://en.wikipedia.org/wiki/Forgetting_curve
72. https://hbr.org/2017/04/let-your-call-center-reps-collaborate